The Curious History of Irish Dogs

David Blake Knox

NEW ISLAND

THE CURIOUS HISTORY OF IRISH DOGS
First published in 2017 by
New Island Books
16 Priory Hall Office Park
Stillorgan
County Dublin
Republic of Ireland

www.newisland.ie

PRINT ISBN: 978-1-84840-701-5
EPUB ISBN: 978-1-84840-588-2
MOBI ISBN: 978-1-84840-589-9

British Library Cataloguing Data.
A CIP catalogue record for this book is available from the British Library.

Typeset by JVR Creative India
Cover design by Anna Morrison

Printed by PUP Introkar, Poland, www.introkar.com

10 9 8 7 6 5 4 3 2 1

For Deborah Spillane,
who knows how to raise pups
of both the human and canine varieties.

Contents

Acknowledgements   ix

Introduction   1

Show Business   13

The Celtic Mist: Irish Wolfhounds   29

Resurrection   40

Rebellion: the Kerry Blue Terrier   62

Counter-Revolution   74

The Original: the Irish Red and White Setter   82

Scandal   97

Little Big Dog: the Glen of Imaal Terrier   106

Whiptail: the Irish Water Spaniel   119

Amber Eyes   126

Daredevil: the Irish Terrier   134

True Grit   141

The Sweetest Music: the Kerry Beagle   149

Stopping the Hunt   155

'War of the Scissors': the Irish Soft-Coated
Wheaten Terrier   164

Our American Cousins   173

'The Only Dog for Ireland': the Irish Red Setter   180

Show and Field   190

Old Dogs   200

New Tricks   207

Acknowledgements

First of all, I would like to acknowledge the assistance given to me in writing this book by the Irish Kennel Club, and in particular by its president, Sean Delmar, who was also kind enough to provide me with photos from the club's archives. The club has a justified reputation not only for its professional expertise and high standards, but also for preserving its non-sectarian and inclusive character through dark periods in Irish history when that may have been difficult to maintain.

I am grateful to all those devoted owners who have spoken to me about their dogs, whether they are kept as family pets, or worked in the field, or exhibited in the show ring. I appreciate those who have given me permission to use pictures of their dogs, or have allowed me to take my own photos. In particular, I should like to thank Frank Hughes from County Tyrone, who provided a photo of his Wheaten Terrier pups; Evan and Bob Devlin, of the O'Dobhailien kennel in Minnesota, USA, for providing photos of their Red and White Setters; Klára Eichacker from the Czech Republic for her photo of Wheaten Terrier pups; Xalibur's Irish Wolfhounds, in Belgium, for the photo of a Wolfhound pup; Mike O'Dwyer and Mike Irving in County Tipperary for allowing me to use a photo and to photograph their Kerry

Beagles; and finally Kenneth Kennedy, a champion breeder in County Wexford, who allowed us to photograph two of his litters, including some of the finest Irish Red Setter pups that I have ever seen.

I am also grateful to Professor Tom Inglis, who brought a sociologist's perspective to our stimulating discussions about the role played by dogs in Ireland over the centuries. I must also mention Tom's Wheaten Terrier, Pepe: a beautiful and sweet-natured bitch whom I have known for almost two decades, and whose picture is included in this book. I am grateful to Dr Michael Cussen, who read some of the early chapters, and whose critical comments were, as usual, much appreciated. I am grateful to my friend Maurice Earls, from the *Dublin Review of Books*, who brought a historian's eye to bear, and who was also most encouraging. I should like to thank Roisín Scully, who read some of the early drafts and gave her informed opinion.

I am grateful to all my children for their advice and support over the years. They have grown up with dogs, and have often recommended articles and books for my attention. My daughter Sarah, in particular, proved indispensable in tracking down rare archive prints and photos, and liaising with owners in Ireland and beyond. She also took some of the photos included in this book. Her mother, Deborah Spillane, has a wonderful understanding of canine psychology, and also knows how to care for dogs properly.

Finally, I would like to record my thanks to all those at New Island for their advice and enthusiasm. In particular, I should like to thank Edwin Higel, Dan Bolger and Justin Corfield for all their valuable suggestions and support. It should go without saying that the responsibility for any errors which the text may contain rests with me.

The book that follows is about Irish dogs—or, to be more precise, about Ireland's native canine breeds. As it happens, the majority of dogs currently living on this island do not belong to any of those breeds. However, this book is focused on the dogs that have been recognised for many years as native to this country. I hope it will show that the histories of those breeds also reveal a good deal about the human beings with whom they have shared the island.

Introduction

The Eikon Centre near Belfast has been described as 'the pinnacle of Northern Ireland's exhibition industry'. I don't know what the competition was like, but the Eikon is certainly one of the largest buildings of its kind on the island of Ireland, with more than 5,000 square metres of space that can be used to accommodate a range of trade events, product launches, conferences and livestock shows. It is, in effect, a huge warehouse that stands like a concrete island bordered on all sides by vast expanses of tarmac parking lots—most of which were occupied on the day I visited the centre.

I had come to attend the Bangor and North Down Combined Canine Club 13th All-Breed Championship Dog Show, to give its full title, which was the club's biggest event to date. Over 1,000 dogs were being exhibited, representing more than 170 different breeds. Inside, the centre was full to capacity, and the show rings spilled out to include a grassy area beside the main hall, where the setters, retrievers and other gun dogs were being shown. It was impossible not to be impressed by the huge variety of breeds that were being exhibited—everything from the pocket-sized short-coated Chihuahuas to the huge Bernese Mountain Dogs. Most of them were familiar to me, but there were some that I had never seen before, such as the Black Russian Terrier (which is not really a terrier at all); the Havanese (the favourite dog of Charles Dickens); and the Keeshond (which, it seems, is also known as the 'Smiling Dutchman').

Inside the centre, there were the usual fevered attempts by owners to make last-minute adjustments to the styling and presentation of their dogs. One of my daughters was with me, and as we passed one adorable Bedlington Terrier bitch, she could not resist petting her. 'Don't do that!' snapped the owner. He whipped out a grooming comb and immediately began to tease the little dog's coat back into shape. My daughter looked as though she wanted the ground to open up and swallow her.

As we walked from one ring to another, it was clear that owners had come to the show from every corner of Ireland. What was equally clear was the pride that each took in their own particular breed of dog. When I commented on the similarities in appearance between the purebred Wheaten Terrier and the crossbred Labradoodle, one owner was quick to inform me that the two dogs were quite different. 'The Wheaten may look a little like that designer dog,' she sniffed, 'but they have very different coats. Besides, the Wheaten is a terrier, and has all of a proper terrier's instincts.' Of course, she was right. The coat of the Wheaten is soft and flowing, while the Labradoodle usually has an abundance of tight curls. In any case, appearance has never been the sole determining feature of any dog breed, and whatever else they might be, Labradoodles are not terriers.

Ireland has one of the highest rates of dog ownership in Europe, and our small island is now home to canine breeds from all over the world. There are hundreds of pedigree dog shows in Ireland every year, with over 200 clubs, associations and societies that are dedicated to preserving and promoting different types and classes of dog. That pales in comparison with the United States, which stages thousands of annual breed shows. Among all the varieties on exhibition, there are nine breeds that can be claimed as native to Ireland. Four of these are terriers: the Irish, the Irish Soft-Coated Wheaten, the Kerry Blue and the Glen of Imaal. There are three gun dogs: the Irish Red and White Setter, the Irish Red Setter and the Irish Water Spaniel. Two of Ireland's native breeds are hounds: the Kerry Beagle and the Irish Wolfhound.

There are a number of other ways in which these nine dogs can be sub-divided and categorised, but perhaps the most telling is that six of the nine breeds are now rated as 'vulnerable' or 'endangered' by kennel clubs in Ireland, the United Kingdom and the United States. According to Sean Delmar, president of the Irish Kennel Club, only around 10 per cent of dogs registered with the club now come from Ireland's native breeds. He believes there is a simple explanation for the decline in their popularity: a 'bigger menu' is now available for dog-lovers to choose from. Thanks to the internet, we can view and buy breeds from all over the world, and there is an obvious attraction for many people in exoticism and novelty. This is the context in which six of Ireland's native breeds face the possibility of becoming extinct. That raises an obvious question: does it matter?

Clearly, it doesn't matter to any of the dogs. They are as wonderfully indifferent to their breed's fate as they are to their own appearance, and couldn't care less whether they are described as purebred or mongrel curs. They also share admirably democratic instincts, and do not wonder much about the social antecedents or pedigrees of any animal with which they are able to mate. When it comes to human beings, however, things inevitably get more complicated. As the popularity of numerous genealogy websites and TV series indicates, we are preoccupied with tracing the bloodlines of our own descent, and it seems we are also happy to transfer that concern to another species. In fact, we now investigate the DNA of our pet dogs almost as much as we do our own.

There are those who believe that the selective breeding of any animal is abhorrent. For such individuals, even the mention of purebred dogs can conjure up horrific images of genetic disorders and unnecessary suffering. Organisations like PETA—People for the Ethical Treatment of Animals— maintain that it would have been in the best interest of dogs if 'the institution of pet keeping' had never existed. According to one PETA website, dogs are kept as virtual prisoners in human households, 'where they must obey commands and can only eat, drink and even urinate when humans allow them to'. Some people may find that description difficult to square with the experience of sharing their home with any dog, pedigree or mongrel. In my own case they have seldom proved quite so biddable or acquiescent as PETA seems to believe. Dogs may offer us their unconditional affection, but they often demand as much in return—and I do mean 'demand'.

There are some who argue that it is foolish to spend large sums of money acquiring a pedigree dog when there are so many loveable mutts incarcerated in shelters and pounds who need to be saved before they face their own—and much more imminent—extinction. That argument is hard to contradict while thousands of dogs are still being euthanised every year. However, it may be worth pointing out that many of the dogs languishing in genuine captivity are purebred animals, who may have been abandoned because they were too much trouble, or because the next fad in dog ownership had already arrived. A few years ago the English Bulldog became the breed of choice among Manhattan's fashionable dog fanciers. Despite their rather daunting appearance, Bulldogs are usually gentle and sweet-natured creatures. However, they are often beset by health problems, and this can make them difficult to maintain. In 1999, there were just thirteen Bulldogs in New York that needed to be rescued. By 2013, that number had jumped to 347.

There are those who believe that Ireland's native dogs form an integral part of our cultural heritage, and we ought to take whatever steps are necessary to ensure that each breed is preserved. It is indisputable that these dogs are part of our island's history, and the Irish Kennel Club has been lobbying politicians for many years to declare that the native breeds of Ireland should be accorded heritage status. It is hard to see why that status hasn't yet been granted—especially considering that it wouldn't cost the Irish government any money. At the same time, some of the more extravagant claims made by breeders concerning the ancient and unbroken lineage of their dogs need to be taken with a liberal pinch of salt. We can only trace the descent of most breeds with confidence for the last 200 years or so, and even within that period of time, many of them have undergone significant changes in appearance and temperament.

Without doubt, there are many breeders who have devoted a great deal of their time and commitment to ensuring that Ireland's native dogs should survive and prosper. One has only to attend any breed show in Ireland to become aware of the genuine devotion that has been lavished on these dogs. The vast majority of Irish owners have done their utmost to maintain the standards of the native breeds, and to care for their animals. It is true there are also some who have placed their own interests first, or who have closed their eyes to the dangers of excessive inbreeding. However, the bulk of those who keep or breed pedigree dogs are unlikely to make a fortune from them. In some cases, the reverse can be the case. 'The bitch I own only threw one pup in each of her litters,' an owner of Glen of Imaal Terriers told me, 'and the second time, she had to give birth by Caesarian.' He had kept both pups, but had to give up any further breeding because 'the vet's costs were more than I could afford, and I live on a housing estate, so I just didn't have room for any more dogs'.

In the course of my life, I have kept pedigree, crossbred and mongrel dogs. They have all had their own individual characters, and I have related differently to each of them. It may sound pious, but I have felt the same degree of affection for each of them—as well as experiencing similar amounts of frustration, impatience and inconvenience. I am not a dog-breeder, and have never exhibited any of the pets I have owned in any show. To be strictly accurate, there was one exception to that rule, but the failure of our family's dog, Missy, to win a prize at a local church fete seemed to upset my children so much that I vowed I would never repeat the experiment.

Apart from the great pleasure which the company of dogs has given me, there has also been the challenge posed by living in close proximity to a member of a different species. However, I am well aware that not everybody shares my sentiments as far as dogs are concerned. My own grandmother could not understand why some people treated dogs as if they were members of the human family. For her, allowing dogs inside a house made as much sense as permitting any other working animal a similar license. 'Would you invite a pig to sit down at your table and eat with you?' she sometimes asked.

The modern dog-breeding industry was created in the middle of the nineteenth century. It was, in the words of one historian, 'an age known for its gentlemen amateurs', and the breeding of dogs was at first regarded as a suitable hobby for men of means and money. Since then it has become a multinational commercial enterprise that is hugely popular across the world. The intensive breeding of pedigree dogs has also proved to be extraordinarily resilient. It has survived catastrophic crashes in the global economy, when the value of certain breeds dropped as sharply as shares in the stock market. And it has emerged from the devastating impact of two world wars, when, for obvious reasons, the breeding of pedigree dogs virtually ceased in Europe. The sheer (one might say, dogged) persistence with which human beings have continued to keep and breed pedigree dogs in the most testing of circumstances suggests a type of emotional need that is difficult to explain. What is clear, however, is that human beings can develop the most intense feelings of affection for their dogs, which may explain why we refer to them as 'pets'. Sometimes this can be accompanied by a suspicious or cynical view of other humans: 'The better I get to know men,' Charles de Gaulle once remarked, 'the more I find myself loving dogs.' That attitude might be traced back to Cervantes' *Dialogue of the Dogs* in the seventeenth century: the first (though certainly not the last) talking-dog story in Western literature, and one in which the deceits and corruption of humanity are discussed by two virtuous members of the canine species.

It has been mooted that the close relationships we can establish with dogs may lead us to question our own status as human beings, since dogs appear to share many of the traits that we are tempted to regard as uniquely human. On the other hand, Sigmund Freud thought that dogs were fundamentally 'unlike humans' because humans were 'incapable of pure love, and always have to mix love and hate'. I am more inclined to share the attitude of the American humorist Dave Berry: 'You can say any foolish thing to a dog, and the dog will give you a look that says, "Wow, you're right! I never would have thought of that!" '

There was a time when we needed dogs to perform many everyday tasks for us. However, the dramatic growth of dog ownership, which has occurred in most European countries over the past few centuries, has been paralleled by a decline in the number of working breeds. This has been related, in turn, to the growth of urbanisation—since most dogs were originally bred to work in the field. The unconditional affection that dogs offer may compensate to some degree for the break-up of traditional networks of support, such as the Church or extended families, and this might also help to explain why we tend to attribute human characteristics to our dogs.

This is not a recent phenomenon: it dates back at least to ancient Greece. In his *History of Animals*, Aristotle suggested that dogs carried traces of our own qualities and defects, such as:

> mildness or cross-temper, courage or timidity, fear or confidence, high spirits or low cunning, and, with regard to intelligence, something akin to sagacity.

Nowadays, we can often be critical of attempts to anthropomorphise animals, but when we look at dogs we cannot help but see a reflection of ourselves. It is a reflection that comes from the perspective of an entirely different species, and I think it is valuable for that alone.

The close connection that many people feel with dogs, and their many similarities to our own species, may offer some explanation why our treatment of these animals can fluctuate wildly. We are clearly capable of both idealising and demonising them. On one hand, humans have named constellations of stars after our trusted companions, and we have used those to navigate our way in the dark. We have also marketed exquisite diamond-studded dog collars that cost hundreds of thousands of dollars. At the same time, we complain when we are being treated 'like a dog', working 'like a dog', and then moan that the country has 'gone to the dogs'. The Devil was once believed to assume the form of a black dog—the 'Hound from Hell'— and on occasion we have even tried and executed some hapless mutts for witchcraft, heresy and treason.

in 2016, Kirsty Henderson, an animal rights campaigner, was quoted in *Vanity Fair* as dismissing dog breeding as 'discriminatory and senseless'. She pledged that she and her colleagues would not rest 'until breeders [were] no longer creating animals for profit'. She may have a long wait, since pedigree dogs are unlikely to disappear any time soon. Indeed, it is reckoned that the majority of all domestic dogs currently being kept in Ireland and the UK are purebred. The number of pedigree dogs is also growing throughout the world, and so is the number of breeds, as well as the number of dog shows. It seems to me that our first and immediate priority should be to ensure that the health and well-being of these animals receive the maximum protection. While recognising the dangers inherent in selective breeding, it would also be foolish to deny the extraordinary beauty and skills of some pedigree dogs, such as the Irish Red Setter, or to ignore the reality that human intervention and selective breeding helped to create that beauty.

In the case of Ireland, I believe that the role our native dogs have played across the centuries can provide some unexpected insights into the social and political history of our country. Ireland is not wholly exceptional in this regard. Indeed, over the course of the centuries, some breeds of dog have become identified with several national stereotypes, or caricatures, rather in the way that individuals are connected with their pets in the famous opening scene of the Disney animated movie *101 Dalmatians*. The British have been identified with Bulldogs; the Germans with Dachshunds; the Russians with Deerhounds; and the French with Poodles.

This tendency to equate ethnicity with dogs reached an extreme form in the middle of the nineteenth century through the work of the leading American physiognomist Dr James Renfield. He believed there were strong physical similarities between the Irish, as a race, and dogs, as a species. He also believed that these similarities extended beyond mere appearance to the fundamental nature of their respective personalities. In this context it is worth remembering that physiognomy, which claims to be able to assess character through the study of external features, was once taken seriously as a form of scientific enquiry. In his monumental *Comparative Physiognomy*, Renfield wrote:

> Compare the Irishman and the dog in respect to barking, snarling, howling, begging, fawning, flattering, back-biting, quarrelling, blustering, scenting, seizing, hanging on, teasing, rollicking, and you will discover a wonderful resemblance.

He did, however, concede that the Irish were 'good servants if you deal harshly with them, as a master does with his dog'. He cautioned against becoming too familiar, since Irish servants were likely to lay 'their filthy paws upon your clean clothes, as if you were no better than they'. I cannot help wondering if it is only a coincidence that the Irish novelist Bram Stoker gave the name of 'Renfield' to Count Dracula's insane henchman, and described him as 'morbidly excitable', 'disturbed' and 'probably dangerous'.

It isn't necessary to subscribe to Dr Renfield's demented racialism to recognise and accept that particular breeds of dog are the products of specific types of society, or that dogs can learn to adjust to different national characters. And there is little doubt that dogs have long occupied a special place in the Irish psyche. Recent research has found that almost four out of every ten Irish homes contains a dog. Great Britain has the reputation of being the country in which dogs are most highly prized, and that seems a perfectly reasonable assumption: the British did, after all, stage the world's first dog shows. But only two out of every ten British homes contains a pet dog. Perhaps that makes the Irish the real dog-lovers of these islands.

On the other hand, Ireland provides very poor public facilities for dogs and their owners in comparison with other nations. In many European countries, public parks are compelled to provide spaces for dogs to be exercised, but these are seldom found in Ireland. In many parts of Europe, dogs can be seen in cafés, bars and restaurants, which seldom happens in Ireland. We are also one of the principal centres of puppy farming in Europe, where the breeding of pedigree dogs takes place on an industrial scale in what are often appallingly cruel conditions, so we can hardly afford to be complacent about our treatment of any animal.

Most of Ireland's native dog breeds are alleged to be part of an ancient lineage that stretches back in time across the millennia. Since no pedigree records reach that far, we are usually expected to take this on trust, or as a given. While it is undoubtedly true that dogs have lived in Ireland for thousands of years, the formation of most of our native breeds is of much more recent origin, and can be directly connected to the emergence of dog shows in the mid nineteenth century. That is also when properly detailed records of dog pedigrees began. The dog shows that began then were initiated by a privileged social class, the landed gentry of Great Britain and Ireland, and although Irish owners and Irish dogs were involved from the beginning, the roots of this phenomenon do not lie in this country, but in England.

Show Business

The world's first dog show was held in the Corn Exchange of the northern English town of Newcastle in June of 1859. One of those who organised the event was a successful gun manufacturer called William Pape. As well as supplying weapons to armies all over the world, Pape was also involved in gun trials, where Victorian gentlemen would test the worth of their guns by shooting game birds in field events. These events involved dogs—usually English Pointers or Irish Setters—and not surprisingly, Irish sportsmen tended to favour the latter. The ownership of sporting dogs such as pointers and setters had been largely confined to the British and Irish upper classes for centuries. In order to keep a working gun dog, it was advisable first to own a gun, and guns were expensive, so their private ownership tended to be concentrated among the landed gentry, or those who aspired to that status.

Ownership of the larger breeds of dog also tended to be restricted to the social classes that had sufficient space in their homes to accommodate them, and it was not uncommon for gentlemen to own more than one dog. The social provenance of these animals had been copper-fastened by a dog tax introduced in the eighteenth century, which was imposed on anyone who owned two or more dogs, and which was not repealed until 1882. By the middle of the nineteenth century, the landed gentlemen in Great Britain and Ireland, who organised and dominated gun trials, wanted their dogs as well as their guns to compete with each other. They could not have realised that they were opening something of a Pandora's box.

This first modern show in Newcastle was attached to an exhibition of farmyard poultry, which was the main event, and entry to the dog show was limited to pointers and setters. Only male dogs were allowed to enter, and all the exhibitors were men. This may have been because the previous occasions on which dogs had competed were vicious and bloody fights. These usually involved gambling, and were normally held behind public houses, so it was considered inappropriate and unladylike for women to attend. On this occasion, however, the Newcastle contest was entirely peaceful, with thirty-six pointers and twenty-three setters taking part in two separate classes. At that stage there were no breed clubs to draw up exacting standards, and both of these classes featured many different types, shapes and sizes of dog. The winners were determined by two panels of three judges: one for pointers and the other for setters. The winning owner in each class received a valuable prize: one of Pape's beautifully crafted shotguns.

One question that arose at the first dog show concerned the criteria appropriate for choosing a winning dog. Although the first classes were confined to sporting breeds, the dogs could not be judged on their abilities in the field since the competition was being held in the middle of an industrial city. Instead, they were assessed on their overall appearance, and how that might translate to their hunting skills. In other words, from the beginning the judging of show dogs, although well-informed, involved some highly subjective factors. This was to continue in future shows, and led to recurring complaints that the field qualities of pointers and setters were being eroded because they were being bred for their 'good neck, bones and feet', rather than the traditional qualities of courage, intelligence, endurance and a good nose.

Before long, two different types of competition had emerged. On one hand, there were field trials for hunting dogs, which, as the name suggests, took place outdoors, and were designed to test the animals' skills. The first of these took place in 1865, and soon gained its own following. This form of competition was conceived as a sporting activity, which was based in rural Britain and Ireland, and it continued for some time to be dominated by the landed gentry. Dog shows, on the other hand, became more of an urban pursuit. Although sporting dogs continued to take part, the appeal of these shows was able to cross a wider range of social backgrounds, and they were much more of a spectator event, which may explain why they soon attracted a larger following.

The differences between these two types of contest have persisted ever since, and have, at times, led to some intense disputes and controversies. The show ring has certainly contributed to changes in the form and character of many animals that were originally bred to work in the field. It has even contributed to different strains of dog emerging within the same breed. According to David Hancock, a current authority on a range of breeds, this may be caused, in part, by the failure of an urban-based population to appreciate that many dogs were never intended to be kept as pets or companions, 'however good they may be in that role'. Instead, he believes that the form of each breed was decided by its function, and 'not by preference or whim'.

All such concerns lay in the distant future for the organisers of the Newcastle show in 1859. Their principal anxiety seems to have been that their exhibition would lose money (£15 was the projected deficit), but as far as William Pape was concerned this would still have made good commercial sense since it offered him an opportunity to promote and sell his guns. In fairness, Pape was also a genuine and enthusiastic dog-breeder who had raised an acclaimed pack of black pointers of his own. He must have been delighted and amazed when the two-day event in Newcastle was attended by more than 15,000 visitors. A local newspaper reported that the presence of dogs had greatly enhanced public interest in the poultry exhibition. This was a portent of what was to come.

The spectacular success of the Newcastle show was followed by another dog show staged in Birmingham later that year. This time, the event was more ambitious. It boldly proclaimed itself to be the 'National Dog Show', and included other sporting breeds: Retrievers, as well as Clumber and Cocker Spaniels, with separate puppy classes. Altogether, thirty different breeds were shown. Viscount Curzon was the patron of this show, and the whole event was organised by the Earl of Derby's gamekeeper, a clear endorsement of its status by Britain's shooting and hunting classes. The event was also hugely successful, and so another was planned for the following year. That also took place in Birmingham, and there were more than 250 entries.

Some of the dogs came from Ireland, and, as it happens, two of the Irish owners were relatives of mine. William Hutchinson won in Birmingham in 1864 with an Irish Setter called Bob (who would later become a famous sire), and the following year his cousin Harry Blake Knox won with Bob's sibling, another all-red Irish Setter called Dan. In 1863, the first major show had taken place in London, in which Bob and Dan had also featured. Bob won the following year at a show in the Cremorne Gardens in Chelsea, which lasted for an entire week. There were 100,000 visitors to that exhibition, including the Prince of Wales, and the event has been described as 'the event of the [social] season'. By 1870, the Birmingham event had become so well established and so popular that the local MP called a meeting to discuss the establishment of a central body that would control the breeding and exhibition of dogs throughout the United Kingdom, which, at that time, included all thirty-two counties of Ireland. A few years later, the same MP and twelve other gentlemen met in London and founded the world's first Kennel Club.

This marked a crucial turning point in the development of the modern dog-breeding industry. However, it was not until the 1880s that the Kennel Club introduced the registration of breed dogs. At first this was opposed by owners and breeders, who feared that this development would centralise and increase the power of the club at the expense of their own independence. However, it soon became obvious that it was necessary to differentiate between various breeds and types of dog if judging decisions were to be consistent and if the shows were to be run effectively. Until then, the pedigrees of show dogs had not been accorded any great priority, and even field dogs were sometimes only identified by their sires. That approach had been summed up in the simple phrase: 'a good dog will get a good dog'. The breeds that existed tended to have little uniformity, and it was sometimes hard even to distinguish between different dogs who shared the same name, which often consisted of just one syllable, such as Dan or Bob. Once registration had been introduced, the pedigrees of the various breeds became of central importance, and for more than three decades all Irish purebred dogs had to be registered with the British club if they were to be exhibited in a championship competition.

This change was also reflected in the development of set routines and strict regulations for shows, as well as the introduction of more distinctive names, which often included the kennel where the dog had been bred. All of this coincided with an explosive increase in the number of exhibitions, and by the start of the twentieth century, substantial dog shows were being staged almost every week in Great Britain and Ireland. Nowadays, winning dogs earn the title of 'Ch.', which indicates that they have qualified for a championship event at a 'conformation' show, where the criteria for judging conform to the set standards. The breeder's kennel prefix, expressed in possessive form, precedes each dog's registered name. This registered name normally differs from the dog's 'call name', which is used by its owners to talk to the animal.

One individual played an especially important role in the growing popularity of the dog shows. His name was Charles Cruft. He was not a dog enthusiast—he claimed to prefer cats—but he was in every sense an exceptional and original showman. In time, he would become the P. T. Barnum of the dog show ring, but in 1870 Cruft found his first employment as an office boy with James Spratt, who had just founded a business selling 'meat fibrine dog cakes'. These biscuits were the first type of food that was manufactured specifically for dogs, and they proved to be extremely popular. Cruft was just fourteen years old when he joined Spratt's, but within a few months he had been promoted to become a travelling salesman, a job ideally suited to his extrovert character. This introduced him to the world of sporting kennels, and he began to realise the commercial potential of the connection between feeding products and purebred dogs. Spratt's business expanded into Europe, and Cruft began to travel extensively on the continent, where he made some useful contacts. In 1878 he was invited to organise the canine section of the great Exposition Universelle in Paris. He was still only twenty-two years old.

When he returned to England, Cruft helped to ensure that Spratt's company grew from a single small shop in the London suburb of Islington to become the world's principal producer of dry dog food. His own reputation also grew, and in 1886 he was approached by the Duchess of Newcastle and asked to organise a breed dog show in London. It was called 'The First Great Show of All Kinds of Terriers'. The event attracted almost 600 entries, which were spread across fifty-seven different classes, and it was another enormous success. This encouraged Cruft to leave Spratt's, and to begin a full-time career as a promoter of dog shows. The next shows he organised were all devoted to terriers, but his seventh show, in 1891, was open to all breeds. It was also the first to be branded with his own name. 'Cruft's Greatest Dog Show' was its modest title; with Spratt's Patent Limited as its sponsor.

Initially, Cruft's shows were not popular with those members of the gentry who had dominated dog-breeding in previous decades. For some of those gentlemen, Cruft's exhibitions seemed more concerned with the quantity of dogs shown than with their quality, and he was considered too vulgar in his appeal to broad-based audiences. Indeed, some breeders detested what they saw as Cruft's crass commercialism, his lack of respect for long-standing traditions, and his high personal profile in the popular press. In the eyes of some well-heeled gentlemen, Cruft was a sensationalist who had caused lasting damage to the reputation of their beloved breeds.

It is true that Cruft massaged his attendance figures to bolster the claim that his shows were the world's biggest, and that he marketed himself almost as much as his exhibitions. However, he was not easily deterred by criticism, and he continued to stage large-scale events for the next forty-five years. During that time he showed a consistent flair for publicity and for innovation, even designing special railway carriages in which dogs could be brought to his shows from distant parts of Great Britain. He was also instrumental in setting up a number of breed clubs, and he played a critical role in introducing many new types of dog to compete in his exhibitions. During World War One he continued running his annual show, and on the same scale as before. This was at considerable financial risk, but he still managed to attract large numbers of visitors to the events, even though they were rumoured to be prime targets for Germany's Zeppelin airships. By the time of his death, Cruft had become extremely wealthy. His annual show was attracting more than 10,000 entries, and those exhibiting dogs had included Queen Victoria and Tsar Alexander II.

Since Cruft's death, the dog show he founded has become even bigger business. The event has been owned by the British Kennel Club since 1948, and the intervening decades have seen its expansion on a scale that might have surprised even its founder. It is still the biggest dog show in the world. It now lasts for four days, and is spread over twenty-five acres, five large exhibition halls, and a 7,000-seat arena in Birmingham's National Exhibition Centre. The show currently attracts up to 25,000 dogs, along with their owners, and more than 150,000 spectators. It is no longer described as a mere show but as an 'experience' for those who attend. Although the prizes awarded to the winning dogs are still relatively modest, the benefits in stud fees and sponsorship can be great.

The Irish have maintained a regular presence at the show. The Irish Kennel Club usually runs a booth in one of the exhibition halls; the judges of different classes are often Irish; and so are many of the entries, and not just with Irish breeds. In 2016, the Irish winner of the 'Best of Breed' in the Japanese Chin class was Lee Grogan, a young Dubliner. He described winning as the fulfilment of his 'biggest dream and ambition'.

Most of the pedigree Irish dogs that exist today owe some degree of debt to Cruft's work. For the most part they were developed out of breeds that could already be found in some form in the late nineteenth century. However, in order to be recognised by the Kennel Club each specimen needed to be 'bred true': in other words, each new generation of that breed had to reproduce what were determined to be its essential and defining features. The standards for Ireland's native dogs are set by each of the Irish breed clubs in conjunction with the national Kennel Club. It must be acknowledged that, in order to conform to their description, systematic culling was once regarded as unavoidable. A significant amount of selective inbreeding was also common. This has the capacity, over time, to produce a genetic bottleneck that can make the opening of stud books, which permits outcrossing with other types of dog, become essential if a breed's health is to be maintained.

From the start, dog shows appealed to the Irish public. They were a new and accessible form of entertainment, and they also became symbols of modern and progressive attitudes towards the breeding of all animals. Indeed, the selective breeding of dogs was sometimes explicitly related to Darwinian theories of natural selection (notably by Darwin's cousin Francis Galton), and the artificial selection, as practised by dog-breeders, was viewed by some as an advance on the unplanned and haphazard evolution that had preceded it. It might also be noted that dogs can be thought to practise their own form of culling: when a dam consistently rejects one of her own litter and will not wean the pup. It could be argued that this is the canine way of maintaining the health of a bloodline, and that this has been undermined by the current practice of ensuring that the runts of litters are kept alive.

In the twentieth century, the ideology of selective breeding came to acquire explicit racist connotations when it was applied to human beings. This reached its nadir in the *Lebensborn* movement of Nazi Germany, which sought to raise the birth rate of 'Aryan' children by sponsoring the procreation of 'racially pure and healthy' offspring. To realise that ambition, the Nazis were even prepared to abduct children whose appearance suggested that they might possibly be of 'Aryan' descent. This shameful history has cast a shadow over the very idea of selective breeding. Indeed, author and activist Michael Brandow was recently quoted as claiming that 'breeding pedigree dogs is just eugenics by another name'. However, the showing of purebred dogs has another less problematic dimension: challenging and overcoming what had been considered to be the fixed and immutable boundaries of gender and class. Judged by the standards of the time, these events allowed a wide range of individuals from different social backgrounds to take part in (relatively) friendly competition. By the start of the twentieth century, many thousands of men and women in Western countries were involved in the breeding, showing and viewing of pedigree dogs.

In the early days, shows had been dominated by sporting dogs and their gentlemen owners, but before long these events were no longer the preserve of the landed gentry. Other breeds began to take centre stage, and new types of dog began to appear. Some of these came from the sub-division of existing breeds. Irish Terriers, for example, were accorded their own separate class at an early stage. The Irish Wolfhound began as part of the Foreign Breed class, but also gained its own recognition. There were also imported breeds, such as the Pekinese, and new breeds that had recently been created, such as the Dobermann Pinscher. And, just as new types of dog began to appear on show benches, so did new types of owner. It was claimed that there was room for 'all tastes and pockets' at a dog show, and women had begun to play a much more active role, particularly in the classes reserved for smaller breeds.

In fact, dog-breeding came to attract a number of committed feminists, such as Florence Nagle, an activist in the cause of female suffrage, who bred both Irish Wolfhounds and Irish Red Setters. It may well be that women have an innate advantage over men as dog trainers. Some recent research indicates that dogs are less likely to be defensive or aggressive around them, and it is estimated that a large majority of companion dog trainers are now female. What is more, as we shall see, several remarkable women played a crucial role in establishing and maintaining some of Ireland's native breeds.

In his brilliant satire on the world of dog exhibitions, *Best in Show*, Christopher Guest focused on the owners and trainers of five pedigree specimens. In the movie, four of the nine main human characters are gay. The proportion may be exaggerated, but for many years dog shows have provided a meeting place where sexual preferences are not considered to be an issue. Guest's movie also reveals how the love of dogs can cross a spectrum of social classes, ranging from the yuppie couple who keep a neurotic Weimaraner called Beatrice to the redneck owner of a doleful Bloodhound called Hubert. Guest also satirises the different approaches to dog-breeding on either side of the Atlantic through two TV commentators: one is a patrician Englishman called Beckwith, who speaks with carefully understated authority; the other is a brash and inept American called Buck, who is cheerfully oblivious of his own ignorance.

Dog shows like Crufts may have originated in England (which could explain the quiet assurance of Mr Beckwith), but they soon spread around the world. Paris held its first show in 1863, and the first American event was staged in 1877. The first modern dog show took place in Dublin in 1873, and within a few years the first Irish breed clubs had also been founded. In 1908, the Dublin Canine Association and the Irish Kennel Association combined to form the Irish Kennel Club. However, the new club was only a regional branch of the British Kennel Club, and had no power to set or recognise breed standards. It was not until 1922 that a genuinely independent Irish Kennel Club was formed. For many decades before then, all shows held in Ireland required a special licence from the Kennel Club in England. As we shall see, the foundation of a separate Irish club coincided, and was connected in some respects, with the foundation of an independent Irish state.

The financial potential of dog shows soon became evident, and it did not take long for these events to become major commercial concerns. Champion dogs could be sold for very large sums, or earn lucrative fees at stud, and some shows awarded large cash prizes to the winners. Against that background, it is not surprising that the judging of exhibitions was subject to increasing scrutiny. In the early days of these events, the judges often knew the competitors (they were, after all, part of a relatively small social elite), and in some cases were even related to them. Inevitably, there were allegations of favouritism, or worse. However, judges were not the only ones who were sometimes accused of dubious practices. There were also allegations that breeders were not averse to trying a few tricks of their own. Some of them were supposed to have trimmed more than the hair on their dogs' ears, or faked coat markings with dye. There were even reports of champion dogs being entered under false names. It could be argued that all of these controversies were testament to the rapid growth in popularity that these shows had experienced.

It wasn't just humans who were affected by this development; dog shows also had a significant effect on the lives of all our domestic animals. The shows introduced the concept of pedigree breeds to a wider public, who might have been ignorant until then of the differences between various types of the same species. Over time, the role and status of domestic animals began to change within British and Irish societies. The principal location of dogs had already shifted from rural to urban settings, although this development was much less pronounced in Ireland. The division of the canine world into purebred, crossbreed and mongrel categories also mirrored in its own way the social structure of Victorian Britain, and the existing demarcation lines between its respective classes and hierarchies. This was, after all, the type of society in which, as George Bernard Shaw observed, it was impossible 'for an Englishman to open his mouth without making some other Englishman hate or despise him'.

Dog ownership is sometimes seen as an economic indicator. The theory is that, as incomes rise, more families can afford a pet. However, there are flaws in that argument: Italians, for example, have a higher ratio of dog ownership than the more affluent Swiss. The Irish love of dogs has been a constant factor throughout our history, and has survived both good and bad times. Dogs feature in the ancient Celtic sagas, and there are many references to them in the manuscripts of medieval and Gaelic Ireland. However, the interest in the particular breeds of dog that developed in Ireland in the late nineteenth century can best be considered as a modern phenomenon. It was part of the general growth in the popularity of pet dogs that began in England, but soon came to encompass much of Western Europe and North America.

This growth was given a distinctly Irish complexion because of a number of critical features in our history, and because of social and political conflicts within Ireland's population. From an early stage in the history of modern dog breeding, there has been a tendency throughout Europe to claim that each purebred dog is the rightful heir to an ancient lineage whose origins are obscured by the swirling mists of antiquity. Irish dogs were, and are, no exception to that rule: indeed, they seem to have been particularly prone to attracting such beliefs. One can sometimes gain the impression that every Irish mutt is a direct descendant of a dog that once belonged to a High King of Ireland, or at least used to run after Cú Chulainn, the great hero of Celtic mythology.

After centuries of colonisation, and a history that has featured military defeats, sectarian disputes, political impotence, recurrent famines and massive emigration, it seems quite understandable that Irish Nationalists would seek to fashion an idealised vision of the past. This vision was one that was filled with undaunted warriors, united in a mystical brotherhood, speaking in the sweet and unsullied tongue of the Gael, and accompanied by their fierce but noble hounds.

Curiously, though for very different reasons, similar myths also appealed to some Irish Unionists, particularly to those in the south and west of the country. They represented, in both literal and figurative terms, Ireland's pre-history, when its population could not easily be categorised as Protestant or Catholic, Nationalist or Unionist, and when the impact of such deep divisions still belonged, in some sense, to the future. This allowed Unionists to assert their Irish identity without compromising their own political or religious beliefs.

In *In Praise of Forgetting: Historical Memory and Its Ironies*, American political analyst David Rieff discusses some of the ways in which history is often 'ransacked' to find reasons that can justify contemporary actions:

> Irish history provides a particularly illuminating case study of the uses and misuses of the past in the construction, reconstruction, amendment, and transformation of the collective memory.

That reckoning seems to apply as much to the history of Ireland's dogs as it does to anything else.

There are nine native breeds of dog in Ireland, and in the course of the nineteenth and twentieth centuries, most of them were caught up in some kind of social movement or political controversy. However, none of Ireland's native dogs has enjoyed quite such a complex and contradictory relationship with Ireland as the dog that has become one of our most recognisable icons: the Irish Wolfhound.

The Celtic Mist: Irish Wolfhounds

My grandfather was fond of reciting long narrative poems to me when I was a child. One of his favourites was called *Beth Gelert*. It was written in the early nineteenth century by William Robert Spencer—a distant relative of Princess Diana. His poem purported to tell the true story of some events that had taken place in Wales in the thirteenth century. According to Spencer, Prince Llewellyn once owned a huge Irish Wolfhound named Gelert. The prince loved to hunt, and Gelert was his favourite hunting dog. Spencer famously described him as 'a lamb at home, a lion in the chase'. One morning, Llewellyn could not find Gelert, and had to hunt without him. When he returned to his castle, Llewellyn was horrified to see that the hound was covered in blood. The cradle in which he had left his infant son had been overturned, and was also drenched in blood. Llewellyn at once assumed that Gelert had killed his son. 'Hell-hound! my child by thee devour'd!' the distraught father cries out in Spencer's poem. He then plunges his 'vengeful sword' into the hound's side. At that moment a child calls out, and Llewellyn discovers his son hidden under some bedding, completely unharmed.

Beside him lies the body of an enormous wolf. It had clearly been killed by Gelert to protect the child, and it was the wolf's blood that had led Llewellyn to imagine the worst. Stricken by remorse, the Welsh prince buried Gelert with honour, and placed a stone above the grave explaining the circumstances of the dog's death. So great was his guilt over killing Gelert that Llewellyn was said never to have smiled again.

This poem made a considerable impression on me as a child, and in particular Spencer's description of Gelert's 'dying yell' struck me as unbearably poignant. When he reached that point, my grandfather usually needed to clear his throat, and I was further moved to see how affected he was by the death of the faithful hound. A dog had displayed exemplary strength, courage and fidelity, but his trust had been betrayed by a human. Many years later it seemed that my own trust, and that of my grandfather, in the truth of this story had also been abused. The legend is apparently of relatively recent manufacture, and is a work of total fiction. It had been invented by a Welsh innkeeper called David Pritchard, who was anxious to drum up business. He even went to the trouble of erecting a fake medieval headstone, and it appears that poor Spencer, who died destitute, had also been his dupe. In fact, variations of this story (usually known as the 'Martyred Dog' legend) appear all over the world. One version even crops up in Walt Disney's *Lady and the Tramp* when Tramp, the Irish Terrier, saves a baby from a large rat, but is believed to have attacked the child, so is promptly dispatched to the pound.

Perhaps all of that is not so surprising: there is, after all, a long tradition in Ireland, and elsewhere, for that matter, of preferring a romantic legend to the more prosaic reality. And none of Ireland's native breeds of dog has been more prone to popular mythologising than the Irish Wolfhound. From an early stage, the size, power and grace of this breed made it stand apart from all others. At the same time, the origins of the Wolfhound, and even the right to claim that name, have been the subject of intense dispute, and the dog's role in Irish history has sometimes been caught up in wider political controversies. Often, it has proved extremely difficult to disentangle the myths from each other.

There are many accounts of great hounds in Irish mythology. In Celtic Ireland, ownership of dogs was governed by social status, and Wolfhounds were only permitted to be kept by the aristocracy. Fionn mac Cumhail, the leader of the mythical Fianna warrior caste, was clearly near the top of that social ladder since he was said to be the master of more than 300 dogs. Two of his favourites were called Bran and Sceolán. They were siblings who could also boast a human descent. Their mother had been turned into a hound while she was pregnant by a woman of the *Sidhe* (the spirit world), who was her rival in love. Bran was described as 'ferocious, white-breasted, sleek-haunched, with fiery deep black eyes that swim in sockets of blood'. His sister, Sceolán, was 'small-headed, with the eyes of a dragon, claws of a wolf, vigour of a lion, and the venom of a serpent'.

Perhaps the best-known Irish legend that involves a great hound is that of Cú Chulainn. The boy Setanta arrived at the court of the High King of Ulster, but before he could enter was attacked by an enormous hound that was keeping guard. Setanta killed the massive dog by driving a *sliothar* (the ball used in hurling) down its throat and smashing its head against a rock. To compensate its owner for the loss, he offered to take its place. He also took the name of Cú Chulainn—'the hound of Culann'. The hero of the Ulster sagas is later credited with having killed an 'unaccountable horde' of dogs in battle.

The war dogs used by the Celtic tribes of Europe acquired an international reputation for their ferocity as well as their size. They are mentioned by Julius Caesar in the account of the Gallic wars, which he wrote in the first century BC. In the fourth century AD, the Roman Consul Quintus Aurelius Symmachus was given seven Irish Wolfhounds. He sent them to the arena to fight with lions, bears and gladiators, where, he reported, 'all Rome viewed them with wonder'. Along with the Wolfhounds' reputation came a growing popularity both within Europe and beyond.

These gigantic dogs became a trophy possession, rather like owning a top-of-the-range Ferrari nowadays, and over the centuries they were sent from Ireland as gifts to a succession of kings, emperors, moguls, shahs, cardinals, ambassadors, papal nuncios and chancellors, as well as assorted princes, lords and grandees. Indeed, so many hounds were sent abroad over the centuries it led one observer to believe it was a reason 'why this noble creature has grown so scarce among us'.

Although Wolfhounds were known for their fierce nature, there are also many Irish stories that relate the gentler side of their character, and the breed seems to have made something of a habit of befriending Irish saints. It was even claimed that Ireland's national saint had a special connection with the Wolfhound. It appears that Saint Patrick once came unexpectedly upon a pagan Irish prince who was hunting with his favourite Wolfhound. The dog's first instinct was to attack the saint, but when Patrick muttered a blessing the Wolfhound fell to the ground and licked his outstretched hand. The Irish prince was so impressed that he immediately converted to Christianity, and Patrick sealed the deal by promising that the Wolfhound would be waiting faithfully for the prince when he arrived at the gates of heaven.

Myths and legends apart, there is no doubt that a large and fierce dog was bred in Ireland many centuries ago, and the reasons for that are not hard to fathom. Celtic clans lived in societies that were both pastoral and warlike. The herds of livestock that belonged to these clans were under constant threat of raids from their neighbours, and from marauding packs of wolves. Clearly, there was a need for the type of fearsome dog that could protect each clan from enemy warriors or wolves, and the Wolfhound was bred to be used in both capacities.

One of the first reliable descriptions of an Irish Wolfhound comes from a Jesuit priest. In the *Historie of Ireland* that he wrote in 1570, Saint Edmund Campion identified the dog as an 'Irish Greyhound', and described it as 'bigger in bone and limb' than a young colt. The Wolfhound was also identified as a 'Wolf-dog', and the different nomenclature can sometimes lead to confusion. What is clear is that the animal we now call the Wolfhound was one of the group of dogs that are known as 'sight hounds'. As the name suggests, these breeds, which include Borzoi, Deerhounds, Salukis, Afghans and Greyhounds, use sight rather than scent to find and follow their prey. Typically, they possess a lean body, deep chest and long legs. They are distinct from other breeds of hunting dog, and subdue their quarry by their speed, stamina and strength. Put simply, a Wolfhound had to be fast enough to overtake a wolf, and powerful enough to kill one.

There are few recorded instances of wolves attacking humans in Gaelic Ireland, and, amazingly, there is even credible evidence that tame wolves and Wolfhounds were sometimes kept by the same owner. However, there is also a good deal of proof that there were large numbers of wolf packs spread throughout Ireland for many centuries, and wolf hunts were a frequent and a popular occurrence. As Dick Warner notes, the customs authorities in medieval Ireland kept good records of the export of animal skins, and these establish that, throughout the sixteenth century, hundreds of wolf pelts were sent every year to England. Given that not all of the skins of wolves killed in Ireland were exported, I think it is safe to deduce that there were a lot of wolf hunts, and a lot of wolves.

Despite the regular and extensive killing of Irish wolves, they survived well into the seventeenth century. As late as 1652, a large wolf hunt took place in Castleknock, now a leafy suburb in the north-west of Dublin City. Nonetheless, by then the fate of Irish wolves was already sealed, and the person most responsible for their ultimate demise was Oliver Cromwell. When Cromwell and his Model Army arrived in Ireland, they were taken aback to find the number of wolf packs that still roamed the country, since wolves had been extinct in England for more than a century. Cromwell may have wished to send the rebellious Irish 'to Hell or Connacht', but he had even grimmer plans for Ireland's wolves. His government placed a bounty on wolf pelts that was far in excess of their previous value, and which soon attracted bounty hunters who went about their business with a new sense of urgency, purpose and ruthlessness.

The settlers that Cromwell had planted in Ireland also engaged in the large-scale destruction of Ireland's forests, chopping down large swathes of what had been the principal habitat of Ireland's wolf population. Within a few years, the number of Irish wolves began to decline rapidly and dramatically. There is some disagreement as to when the last surviving Irish wolf was hunted down, but the final authenticated case was in 1786, when a sheep farmer in County Carlow tracked one back to his lair on Mount Leinster, where the lone wolf was killed by his dogs. By then there had been very few wolves on the island for many decades, and by the end of the eighteenth century the Irish wolf had become completely extinct. As Dick Warner has commented, if any of the genes of native wolves can still be found in Ireland, they exist only through previous interbreeding with our domestic dogs.

Ironically, the Cromwellian Plantation, which spelled doom for Ireland's wolves, had initially boosted the number of Irish Wolfhounds. In April of 1652, Cromwell's government in Kilkenny decreed that it was an offence to export 'wolfe dogges' from Ireland. The decree began:

We are credibly informed that wolves doe much increase and destroy many cattle in several partes of this dominion, and that some do attempt to carry away such great dogges, as are commonly called wolfe dogges.

Those dogs were shipped to England, where they could be sold for large sums. Cromwell noted that such animals were 'useful for the destroying of wolves', and if their export continued, his plans to rid Ireland of wolves would 'speedily decay'. Consequently, he instructed his customs officials to seize 'all such dogges' that were being taken out of the country. Despite that prohibition, Cromwell's son, Henry, who was a member of the Irish Council of State, still managed to sneak some Wolfhounds out of Ireland for his English friends.

The extinction of Irish wolves had obvious and ominous implications for the future of the dog that had been bred primarily in order to hunt and kill them. As the eighteenth century progressed, the decline in the number of Irish Wolfhounds began to parallel that of their former prey. References to the Wolfhound still pay tribute to its size and graceful shape, but increasingly they also refer to its scarcity. In 1774, the Irish novelist, poet and playwright Oliver Goldsmith published his wonderful compendium, *A History of the Earth, and Animated Nature*. In its eight volumes Goldsmith covers a great deal of ground, from 'mines and mineral vapours' to 'winds, irregular and regular', seeking to combine detailed biological descriptions with complex emotional responses to the natural world. The section entitled 'An History of Animals' includes a lengthy and deeply ambivalent discussion of the 'great Irish Wolfdog', which he regarded as the 'most wonderful' breed and 'the first of the canine species'.

Goldsmith declared a personal connection with this dog, claiming that his mother's life had been saved by a Wolfhound from a ferocious attack by a wolf. He describes the breed as 'extremely beautiful and majestic as to appearance'. He also acknowledges, however, that the dog is 'very rare even in the only country in the world where it is to be found'. According to Goldsmith, the ancient Irish hound was now 'kept for show [rather] than use' because there were 'neither wolves nor any other formidable beasts of prey in Ireland that seem to require so powerful an antagonist'. Goldsmith suggests that the animal had merely become a kind of 'curiosity' that is 'bred up in the houses of the great'. This theme of a redundant purpose is reinforced by Goldsmith's assertion that the Wolfhound is 'neither good for hunting the hare, the fox, nor the stag, and equally unserviceable as a house dog'.

Goldsmith claimed to have seen around a dozen purebred Wolfhounds in his lifetime, and it is clear that he regarded their decline as one that involved more than mere numbers. He believed that the dog's moral character had also grown 'heavy and phlegmatic'. This he attributed to Wolfhounds 'having been bred up to a size beyond [their] nature'. Their owners had taken 'the greatest pains to enlarge the breed, both by food and matching', but had achieved their goal, he believed, 'at the expense of the animal'. Goldsmith saw little future for the breed:

> They were once employed in clearing the island of wolves, which infested it in great plenty; but these being destroyed, the dogs are also wearing away, as if nature meant to blot out the species, when they had no longer any services to perform.

This passage reminds me of some the themes which Goldsmith had explored a few years earlier in *The Deserted Village*. That poem laments the collapse of a vibrant human community that had once seemed fixed and stable, just as the Wolfhound had once seemed a permanent feature of Irish life. There is a sense that Ireland, in Goldsmith's eyes, has lost its Wolfhounds just as the deserted village in his poem has lost its people. In both cases, dogs and humans have seemed powerless to change their destiny, and have moved inexorably towards their own extinction. In both cases there is the prospect of an even bleaker future—according to Goldsmith, only 'half the business of destruction' has been done. And in both cases it is tempting to conclude that Goldsmith was strongly influenced by the depopulation of that part of rural Ireland that he had observed growing up, and by the notion that a proud and heroic past had been discarded and forgotten.

Writing fifteen years after Goldsmith, Richard Gough, a British naturalist, categorised the Irish Wolfhound as a type of Greyhound that was 'remarkably large and peculiar to the kingdom of Ireland'. He went on to state that 'this race [of dog] is now almost extinct; there are not, perhaps, ten in the country'. The following year, Thomas Bewick, another British naturalist, thought the 'Irish greyhound' to be 'the largest of the dog kind, and its appearance the most beautiful'. However, Bewick also noted that the breed 'is only to be found in Ireland, and is now extremely rare'.

By the early nineteenth century, the few remaining dogs that were identified as genuine Irish Wolfhounds were invariably said to be 'the last of their race'. It seems unlikely to me that many of these could have been purebred Wolfhounds. Given the very small numbers, it appears inevitable that some cross-breeding must have occurred. As early as 1750,

Lord Chesterfield had complained that he had been trying for several years to obtain 'those large dogs of Ireland'. When he finally managed to secure two, he discovered to his dismay that 'a mixture of the Danish breed' had compromised their bloodlines. Nonetheless, even as their numbers fell, Wolfhounds still managed to retain an iconic status in their native country. Daniel O'Connell, the Irish nationalist leader, was often painted in the company of a large hunting dog, as if to remind any viewers that he was descended from ancient Gaelic nobility. In time, the Wolfhound would become as ubiquitous a symbol of Old Ireland as the Harp of Brian Boru, the Round Tower or the Celtic Cross. Indeed, these four were often depicted together as remnants of a distant past.

However, in May of 1841 an article was published in the *Dublin Penny Journal* by someone who signed himself 'HDR'. The anonymous author made a startling claim: not only did he believe that the Wolfhound was not extinct, but he believed that the breed was alive and well and living in Scotland.

Resurrection

The author who signed himself 'HDR' was a Scottish former British Army officer called H. D. Richardson, who had retired to live in Ireland with the intention of breeding dogs. In this article, Richardson claimed that no other animal had 'attained an equal amount of fame, or excited an equal degree of attention' throughout the world as the Irish Wolfhound. He pointed out that the breed continued to command interest and respect even though it was now 'considered to be extinct'.

Richardson argued that, in fact, the authentic bloodlines of the ancient Wolfhound still existed. He believed that they had been taken to Scotland many centuries earlier by immigrants from Ulster. He also believed that the Irish Wolfhound was so intimately related to the current Scottish Deerhound breed as to be almost indistinguishable—although he reckoned that the latter lacked the physical substance of the original hound. Richardson elaborated his theories in a book published a few years later, and soon afterwards he used Deerhounds crossed with other large breeds to produce a dog that he thought closely resembled 'the true appearance and form of the ancient Irish wolf-dog'.

It has to be said that not everyone was convinced by Richardson's arguments. Although his audacious claims were delivered with supreme self-confidence, they were not supported by very much hard evidence. The reviewer in the English journal *Punch* suggested that, while many fantastical stories were hard to credit, if anyone were convinced by Richardson's highly coloured account, then all others would be easy for them to swallow. However, more than twenty years after Richardson's article was published, an Englishman reached similar conclusions, and he was also determined to restore the Wolfhound breed to its former glory. Captain George Augustus Graham was to devote the next half-century of his life to that mission, and he may be considered, with good reason, to be the founder of the modern Irish Wolfhound breed.

Like Richardson, Graham had served as an army officer. As a young man he had joined the East India Company's Bengal Infantry, and while serving in India had helped to suppress the great mutiny of 1857. Graham was clearly of a romantic disposition. Although he was born and raised in England, his family was of Scottish origin, and he liked to dress in the full Highland regalia of the Graham clan. In later years he grew a white goatee beard, and his general appearance was not unlike Colonel Sanders of Kentucky Fried Chicken fame.

As a youth, Graham had collected the pedigrees of Scottish Deerhounds. However, when he retired from active military service, Graham turned his attention to the Irish Wolfhound, and bought a large estate in rural Gloucestershire to provide sufficient room for his ambitious breeding plans. For the next half-century, Graham may have seemed to follow the lifestyle of an archetypal Victorian country gentleman. He served on the bench as a magistrate. He was chairman of the parish council. He was a stalwart of the Conservative Party. He contributed to local charities, and he supported the village cricket team. But for all those years, Graham maintained one constant and overriding passion: to bring the Irish Wolfhound back to life.

As Richardson had observed, there was no agreement about how Wolfhounds had once looked, so Graham claimed to have studied old books, poems, drawings and paintings. It has to be said that these early depictions of the Wolfhound do not bear much resemblance to the specimens that Graham eventually bred. Nonetheless, he did arrive at a firm idea of how he conceived the ideal Wolfhound, and he even had a life-size model of the dog constructed which reproduced that image. He then attempted to create its likeness in flesh and bone: a remarkable example of life literally imitating art. Graham was convinced that there were still some specimens of the old bloodlines available in Ireland, and from 1863 he set about advertising for them. At first he did not meet with much success, but eventually he was able to acquire some, and to claim proudly that 'their blood is now in my possession'.

However, Graham was not fully satisfied with the Irish dogs he had obtained. Some of them proved to be infertile, and he was disappointed by the size and shape of most of the pups that the others produced. Graham wanted to breed authentic Irish Wolfhounds, but given the very small number of dogs that could claim some degree of genuine ancestry, it was clearly necessary for him to outcross his specimens. He drew primarily upon Deerhounds and Borzoi, but it seems that English Mastiffs and even a Tibetan Kyi Apso also contributed to the gene pool. In order to fix the standard features of the breed, Graham felt compelled to practice some very close breeding, and to mate dogs and bitches from the same litter. This degree of in-breeding may explain why Graham later acknowledged that 'death and disease' had taken most of his 'finest specimens'.

Despite the setbacks, Graham persevered, and in 1879 he persuaded the Kennel Club to include a class of Wolfhounds in its annual Dublin show. However, the name of the class in which they were exhibited revealed a considerable degree of caution on the part of the show's organisers; it bore the awkward title of the 'Nearest Approach to the Old Irish Wolfhound'. Graham, who acted as judge, was disappointed by the quality of the dogs entered, and by the considerable variations in their appearance. Some of those shown had previously taken part in the Deerhound class, and in his judge's report Graham described the winning entry as 'a Deerhound of unusual size'. However, he also stated his belief that this dog 'needed nothing more than bone and substance to be our ideal of an Irish Wolfhound'.

By then, Graham felt sufficiently confident of the progress he had made in his own breeding programme to publish a monograph, *The Irish Wolfhound*, in which he set out his understanding of the origin and development of the dog that he regarded as the 'king of the canine race'. He began by admitting that the Wolfhounds he had bred did not embody the dog 'in its original integrity', but he then cited the previous claims of Major Richardson as evidence that the Scottish Deerhound was a direct descendant of the Irish Wolfhound—although, like Richardson, he believed that 'the Irish dog was far superior in size and power'. He also referred to the recent archaeological discoveries of canine skulls by 'Surgeon Wylde' (Oscar Wilde's father), which appeared to support his view.

Graham included his own detailed description of the Wolfhound's 'general appearance and character', and asserted his right to pronounce with authority on this matter. He had, he claimed, 'not only studied the subject carefully, but [had] bred extensively'. He acknowledged that, due to endemic disease, he had already 'lost all the finest' of his Wolfhounds. Yet his convictions remained unshaken, and he declared that he was secure in 'the very certain knowledge' that it was still 'perfectly possible to breed the correct type of dog'. Graham's monograph concluded with a stirring exhortation to his readers:

Of all dogs the monarch and the most majestic—
shall he be allowed to drop from our supine grasp?
Irishmen!—Englishmen!—all ye who love the
canine race—let it not be so.

The monograph was revised and reprinted in 1885 to coincide with Graham's foundation of the Irish Wolfhound Club. On this occasion his pamphlet attracted some adverse comment in the pages of *The Field* illustrated magazine. *The Field* was then, and remains, the world's oldest country and field sports magazine. It was founded in 1853, and had taken advantage of the growing market for the type of 'gentleman's literature' that featured articles about field sports, dog trials and gun reviews. It also gave extensive and vivid coverage to Britain's colonial wars, which it usually treated as if they were also sporting events. From the start, the magazine proved a huge success, and was highly influential.

In an editorial of June 1885, *The Field* damned Graham's monograph with faint praise. It recognised the 'considerable pains' that the author of the work had taken, and acknowledged that it contained some 'interesting, if not original' information. However, *The Field* could discern no basis for Graham to claim that any of the Wolfhound's original bloodlines had survived. 'So far as our impressions went,' *The Field* commented, 'this [breed has] been extinct for some time, probably a century.' Graham had included photographs of his two favourite Wolfhounds in his pamphlet. *The Field*'s wounding verdict was that 'the appearance of neither is elegant', and the magazine predicted that the new Irish Wolfhound Club, which Graham had just founded, would fail since there were so many genuinely purebred dogs that were 'more handsome, and quite as useful'.

Graham responded to *The Field*'s comments in the following edition. He pointed out that he had never claimed that a 'true strain' of the Wolfhound was still in existence, but at the same time he remained convinced that 'more or less true and authentic blood' could be found. That may seem like a fine distinction, if not an obvious contradiction, but Graham remained resolute in his belief that he could identify a genuine Wolfhound bloodline, and this would be the foundation on which the old breed might be rebuilt in its 'correct form'. In a final defiant gesture, he suggested that the restored Wolfhound would not be 'any more manufactured than has been the case with many that are now looked upon as "pure".' In reply, *The Field*'s editor accepted that many purebreds had been crossed 'to arrive at their present form', but continued to question whether

Captain Graham's Wolfhounds could be traced 'in any line' back to the original breed.

Graham's monograph was also criticised by Hugh Dalziel, author of the well-regarded *British Dogs*. His tone was less condescending than that of *The Field*, but he also reckoned that the blood connection between Graham's dogs and the original Wolfhound breed was 'infinitesimal'. He argued that Major Richardson, from whom Graham had obtained specimens, had failed to establish that the strain of dog he had bred contained any 'pure Wolfhound blood' in its veins. While he was prepared to accept that Graham might succeed in producing a 'gigantic rough-coated dog', he suggested that this could be achieved only through a 'large addition of foreign blood'. In his view, this made Graham's goal, which was the 'resuscitation of an ancient race', quite impossible.

However, Graham was not only dedicated to his breeding programme, he was also skilful at publicising his work, and he was able to recruit a number of enthusiastic disciples to his cause. These included A. J. Dawson, the author of a novel called *Finn—The Wolfhound*. His book was given to me by my grandfather when I was about nine years old, and I promptly fell in love with its dog-hero. The novel tells the story of a huge purebred Wolfhound, an outstanding specimen, and a champion of champions. Dawson relates how Finn is stolen from his master in Australia. The dog survives all sorts of trials and tribulations—exhibited in a circus as a dangerous animal, and leading a pack of wild dingos in the outback—before he is finally reunited with his master.

The graphic descriptions of Finn's abuse in the circus would probably be thought wholly unsuitable for young children nowadays: we live, after all, in an era when Enid Blyton's tyrannical teacher, Dame Slap, has been renamed as 'Dame Snap', and now administers only verbal abuse and not corporal punishment to her unfortunate pupils. However, when I read the novel as a child, I must confess that I found it thrilling as well as terrifying. Throughout all his ordeals, Finn is shown to be brave, strong, wise, kind, resourceful and loyal—all the virtues towards which human beings aspire, but don't always manage to attain. As it happened, the dog reminded me of those qualities that I could see in my own grandfather, and the two almost merged in my childish imagination. The book proved very popular for many years, particularly in the United States. It ran to numerous editions, and greatly increased public awareness of the breed.

Some of Graham's more fervent supporters seem to have viewed the breeding of Wolfhounds in mystical or quasi-religious terms as a form of resurrection in both literal and metaphoric ways. According to Ralph Montagu Scott, an early devotee of the breed, the Wolfhound was:

> supreme among the canine races for intelligence and an almost uncanny sense of good and evil, sublime in his devotion, the joy of his master's heart, and faithful unto death.

Graham also had influential social connections, which helped to ensure that the standards and points of merit he had written for the Wolfhound breed were quickly ratified by the British Kennel Club. He also suggested that Irish Wolfhounds, which had been registered as 'Foreign', should be given their own registration rights. This was accepted by the Kennel Club, and in July 1886, twenty-four Irish Wolfhounds were registered in a new section.

When the Wolfhound Club was founded in the previous year, its first president was Lord Arthur Cecil, son of the Marquis of Salisbury, and uncle of a future British Prime Minister—further evidence of Graham's well-placed connections. Graham served as the Honorary Secretary and Treasurer, and the other club officers were largely drawn from the Irish gentry and landowning classes. A high proportion of these were Protestant in religion and Unionist in their politics. For such people, an interest in Ireland's native dogs, and the remote Celtic past with which they were associated, provided an opportunity to express their own sense of Irish identity without having to abandon their political or religious beliefs. The poet Patrick Kavanagh later took a more sceptical, not to say harsh, view of their position. 'A great many Protestants,' he wrote, 'seeking roots in this country have attempted to build a national myth into a spiritual realty.' Kavanagh believed that their apparent interest in 'Irish horses [and] Irish dogs' was contrived, and only an 'empty distraction'.

As it happened, the Irish Wolfhound Club seemed to have been launched at an opportune time. It coincided with the growth of a number of creative and cultural movements in Ireland that came to be known collectively as the Celtic Revival. The overall goal of this revival was to link Ireland's national identity more explicitly to its Celtic past, although in some cases this involved restoring alleged traditions that were every bit as suspect as the bloodlines of Captain Graham's dogs. Despite that, the Celtic Revival enjoyed a good deal of popular support, and appealed to many interests.

According to Douglas Hyde, who later became the first president of the independent Irish state, the cultural goal of Nationalists should be to 'cultivate everything that is most racial, most smacking of the soil, [and] most Irish'. Hyde led the campaign to return the ancient Irish language to its pride of place. There was also a popular movement to regenerate the ancient Gaelic sports and make them available in every Irish parish. There was a drive to reinvigorate Ireland's old traditions of scholarship and learning, and to make the ancient Celtic sagas accessible to contemporary readers. There was even an attempt to introduce what were imagined to be the costumes and decorative fashions of Celtic Ireland. Against that revivalist background, it may not seem surprising that there was also an attempt to resurrect an ancient Celtic dog, or that the poet W. B. Yeats and playwrights Lady Gregory and J. M. Synge would chose the Wolfhound to be an emblem of the Abbey, Ireland's new national theatre.

Given the practical and financial demands involved in breeding and keeping Wolfhounds, it is understandable that Graham's club established only a relatively modest and fairly affluent following. However, even more popular organisations, such as the Gaelic League, found it impossible to avoid getting caught up in the religious and political divisions that ran through Ireland in the late nineteenth and early twentieth centuries. Despite the wishes of its founders, the Irish Wolfhound Club proved to be no exception to that rule.

By the start of the twentieth century, the Wolfhound Club membership was running low. Rawdon Briggs Lee, later editor of *The Field*, was one of the Wolfhound's most enthusiastic supporters. Although Lee was English, he felt indignant that the breed had not caught the 'popular fancy' in Ireland:

> The natives of the Emerald Isle have refused to answer the call. In the national emblem of Erin, an Irish wolfhound is seen lying beside the Harp, but, as a rule, the prizes for the national breeds [at dog shows] in Dublin are swept away by the Saxon invader.

Lee could not resist pointing out that, if it had been left to the Irish alone, 'this canine relic might now be extinct'. In the spring of 1899, the President of the Irish Wolfhound Club, Lord Caledon, died, and his place was taken by Captain Graham. The members of the Club Executive used the occasion to record their appreciation of Graham's valiant attempts to resuscitate the Wolfhound, acknowledging that he had spent the previous thirty-five years in 'untiring, and for a long time almost unaided efforts' to do so. Although the club only numbered thirty-three members, they were said to remain 'decidedly hopeful' that, under Graham's leadership, the long-term future of the breed would be secured. They did not have to wait long for the new President's first initiative.

On 11 October 1899, the South African Republic, the Transvaal and the Orange Free State declared war on the United Kingdom. In the following months, intense sympathy for the rebellious Boers swept over Nationalist Ireland. Huge demonstrations in favour of Afrikaner independence were held in Dublin, British forces were attacked in the streets, and the Vierkleur—the flag of the Transvaal Republic—was carried through many Irish towns and flown from Irish buildings. Before long, Irish immigrants to South Africa had formed two brigades of volunteers to fight alongside the Boer militias against the British Army. They issued a statement, which read in part: 'England has been a vampire, and has drained Ireland's life-blood for centuries. The time is at hand for revenge.' As Donal McCracken has observed, there was little thought given to the evident incongruity of Irish guerrillas, who were mainly Catholic, joining what was essentially a Calvinist army, and even less for the implications that a Boer victory might hold for South Africa's black or mixed-race populations.

Of course, Irish enthusiasm for the Boer cause needs to be seen in perspective. The number of Irishmen who joined the South African brigades can be counted in hundreds; the number of Irishmen who fought in South Africa as part of the British Army can be reckoned in many thousands. One of these was a relative of mine. Ernest Blake Knox was present at Tugela Heights when Irish soldiers could be found on both sides of the battle lines. Subsequently, he wrote a book about the campaign in which he paid tribute to what he regarded as the remarkable heroism of the Irish regiments, and the large number of Irish soldiers who had been killed in action. When the war was over there had been almost 4,500 casualties in the ranks of the Irish Fusiliers, the Irish Regiment, the Irish Lancers and the Dublin Fusiliers. That compared with a total of just 91 casualties in the Irish brigades that had fought with the Boers.

As McCracken has commented, the losses incurred by the brigades were insignificant when set against those of regular Irish regiments, but it was the activities of the brigades, and not the regiments, which caused excitement back in Ireland. Later, when a triumphal arch was raised in Dublin to the memory of the hundreds of Dublin Fusiliers who had died in South Africa, it quickly became known to radical Irish Nationalists as 'Traitors' Gate'.

For predictable reasons, Captain Graham did not sympathise with the pro-Boer elements in Irish society. Indeed, since he lived in the heart of rural England, he might not have been conscious of their existence. Even if he had been fully aware, it seems most unlikely that he would have understood the complex nuances of Irish politics, which were at that time undergoing both profound and, as R. F. Foster has argued, generational changes.

During the South African War, an Irish general had requested that Irish regiments be allowed to wear shamrock on St Patrick's Day. His request was granted, and his original proposal grew into the idea of creating a new regiment of Irish Guards within the British Army. Graham saw an opportunity, and proposed to the club that a Wolfhound should be presented to the new regiment 'with a view to increasing the popularity of the breed'. The club authorised him to organise a competition with a prize of thirty guineas for the winning dog. Graham's offer was accepted by the guards, and a special class was created at the Kennel Club Show at Crystal Palace in 1902. There were eight entries, and the principal judge was Graham. He awarded the prize to a two-year-old called Rajah of Kidnal (whose un-Irish name was promptly changed to Brian Boru). Since then, a Wolfhound has served as the regimental pet, and subsequently the mascot, of the Irish Guards.

The gift of the Wolfhound generated a good deal of publicity, as Graham had anticipated, and it proved very popular with members of the Wolfhound Club. However, it did not play so well with radical, or 'advanced', Irish Nationalists. They tended to view the Wolfhound as the sort of dog that only members of a privileged elite could afford to own. They were also inclined to presume that such people were probably 'West Brits', or Unionist in their political sympathies. Nationalist disapproval of Graham's initiative became even more pronounced when the First Battalion of the Irish Guards was sent to fight for Great Britain in South Africa. According to Rudyard Kipling, the Irish soldiers were drawn to the sound of guns 'like salmon to the sea'.

When the Nationalist militia, the Irish Volunteers, was formed in 1913, its choice of mascot was still the Wolfhound, but a shift was taking place in the attitude of the younger generation towards the Wolfhound Club, and the breed. Their affections began to move towards some of Ireland's other native dogs, and this may explain why plans were eventually formed to replace the Wolfhound as Ireland's de facto national breed. Some of the issues arising from these disputes were satirised by James Joyce in the 'Cyclops' episode of his great novel *Ulysses*. Most of this rich and complex episode takes place in Barney Kiernan's pub in the centre of Dublin. The unnamed narrator of this episode talks in the racy vernacular of the city streets, but his voice is interrupted repeatedly by parodies of other forms of language and styles of writing. These include the overblown sort that Celtic Revivalists often used to translate, or imitate, the ancient Irish sagas. In Kiernan's pub we meet a radical Irish Nationalist called 'The Citizen', who is also a virulent racist, and who is accompanied by his equally malevolent dog, Garryowen.

This was the name of a famous Irish Red Setter, a champion show-dog who was owned by a dog-breeder called James Giltrap. His daughter, Josephine, had married Joyce's uncle, which means that Joyce was quite closely related to the Giltraps by marriage, and was more than likely aware of both Garryowen and his owner. According to some commentators, this suggests that Giltrap's dog is the real-life model for the dog that appears in this episode. That interpretation may be too literal, and risks missing the point of Joyce's satire. In any case, Garryowen, the real-life setter, had been dead for some years by 1904 (the year in which Joyce's novel takes place), and he is usually accurate about that sort of detail. There are other, and I think more suggestive, ways of understanding what is, for me, the most remarkable dog in modern fiction: there are, after all, very few canine specimens that are able to sing a traditional Irish air.

Garryowen is described by Joyce in the inflated and mock-heroic idiom he uses to parody the Celtic Revivalists. However, he is also described by the unnamed narrator of this episode in much less reverential terms. Indeed, Garryowen is dismissed both as a 'bloody mangy mongrel' and as 'the famous old Red Setter wolf dog', suggesting that his bloodline is, to say the least, far from pure. It is true that the name of Garryowen was attached to a real champion setter. But this was also the title of a drinking song, and a musical air that was closely connected with Irish regiments of the British Army. In particular, the air was associated with a famous incident that occurred during the Napoleonic Wars when the commanding officer of an Irish regiment had used it to encourage his troops to repel an attack by French Grenadiers. The same air was commonly used by contemporary Orange bands, although their lyrics included lines such as 'We'll kick the Pope before us', which were not found in the original.

There was also more than one Irish unit of the British Army that kept a Wolfhound as a mascot. In 1915, when Joyce was writing *Ulysses*, it was widely reported that the Third Battalion of the Munster Fusiliers had been presented with one, and it was also called Garryowen. Against that background, Joyce was clearly satirising the confused and contradictory legacy left in the wake of what he had termed the 'nightmare' of Irish history.

Viewed from this perspective, the 'national dog' of Ireland is, in reality, nothing more (or less) than a mongrel, and the progeny of many different and unknown breeds. In other words, the dog's alleged origins in the mists of Celtic antiquity represent a confused and confusing fantasy, and a doomed attempt to recreate a lost pedigree. The same, it may be inferred, applies to the grandiose ambitions of the Revivalists, as well as to the nonsensical claims about Irish history that are spewed out by The Citizen. As Sam Slote has pointed out, for Joyce, dogs are always mongrels, but it is 'precisely in this mongrelization that they might have some affinity to the Irish'.

When George Graham died in 1909, he was buried, as he had wished, to the 'mournful sound of the Scottish pipes'. He was also eulogised in terms that were so extravagant they might have come from one of Joyce's parodies. Ralph Montagu Scott wrote:

> Captain Graham has left us for the happy hunting grounds, where to be sure he has found his favourite hounds awaiting him. Did not the Irish warrior Oisin say to St Patrick: 'To the sons of Cumhall and the chiefs of the Fianna it is sweeter to hear the voice of hounds than to seek mercy'?

That mourner was, at least, able to find some consolation: he believed that, thanks to Graham:

the spirits of the great hounds of Ireland stalk the earth again, for today the Irish Wolfhound lives and moves and has his being as the Monarch of the Canine World.

Curiously, a similar image of a heroic figure from Ireland's Celtic past, summoned back from the dead, appears in one of Yeats's poems about the 1916 Rising: 'When Pearse summoned Cuchulain to his side,' he wondered, 'What stalked through the Post Office?'

There are two obvious questions to be asked when assessing what Captain Graham achieved in half a century of relentless and dedicated commitment to this breed of dog. The first is whether or not he succeeded in resuscitating the ancient Irish Wolfhound. The second is whether or not it matters.

For me, the answer to the first question must be a reluctant 'no'. I think it most unlikely that many, if any, of the ancient Irish bloodlines can be found in today's Wolfhounds. Although Graham kept detailed records of his breeding programmes, they are based on the assumption that some of the dogs he obtained were genuine descendants of the original breed. Sadly, there seems to be very little evidence of that. As long ago as 1906, the verdict of one respected show judge was that there was 'little or no connection with the past in the wolfhounds now being shown'. In fact, given Graham's extensive use of outcrosses, it seems possible that there is more of the original bloodlines in some of Ireland's other native breeds, such as the Wheaten or Irish terriers, than in the modern Wolfhound.

My answer to whether this matters is also 'no', although this time the answer is given with less reluctance. George Graham was not the sole breeder of Wolfhounds in the course of the nineteenth century, but he was, by far, the dominant one, and in many respects it was his personal aesthetic tastes that determined the final standards of the breed. Until the nineteenth century, the vast bulk of dogs were bred for specific purposes. However, the Wolfhounds bred by Graham were never intended to hunt wolves, or to fulfil any function other than to look like Wolfhounds—or at least, to look like Wolfhounds as they had been imagined by Graham. The standards he set have barely changed in all the decades that have passed since his death, which is in itself a tribute to his founding vision. Graham may not have resurrected the original Wolfhound, but he still managed to design and create a distinctive and very beautiful breed of dog, and one that has now established itself across the world. It is questionable if any sort of Irish Wolfhound would exist today without his extraordinary level of dedication and his unstinting commitment of personal resources.

It is only fair to mention that a price was paid for Graham's determination to create, or recreate, the Wolfhound breed, and much of that price was paid by the dogs themselves. By Graham's own admission, many of the animals that he bred died when they were still very young, probably as a result of his frequent use of extremely close inbreeding. This was, of course, in line with the practice of the time, and Graham also systematically culled those pups which did not conform to his notion of the ideal Wolfhound. He decided, for example, that blue was impermissible as a breed colouring, and all affected pups were put down at birth, or as soon as that colour became obvious.

Thanks to Graham's efforts, the modern Irish Wolfhound is generally reckoned to be the tallest of all sight hounds. As a result, and like most other breeds of giant dogs, Wolfhounds have a relatively short lifespan. Obviously, there are exceptions, but their average length of life is only around seven years. There are other large breeds, such as the Great Dane and Saint Bernard, whose life expectancies are even shorter. Nonetheless, the average life expectancy of a Wolfhound is close to half that of many smaller breeds. The leading cause of death is bone cancer, and, like all deep-chested dogs, gastric torsion, or bloat, is also relatively common.

In the last century, there were times when the future of the Wolfhound in Ireland seemed uncertain. During both world wars, food shortages decimated stock and bloodlines. In their aftermath, breed numbers had fallen so low that sires and dams had to be imported from the United States to replenish them. However, the breed had flourished on the far side of the Atlantic, as it continues to do, and a full recovery was made.

The Wolfhound has managed to retain its iconic status through all the years, and all vicissitudes. Captain Graham may not have known it, but he established a brand as well as a breed, and the image of the Wolfhound, more or less as imagined by him, has featured on bottles of Irish whiskey, pieces of pottery, public monuments, army medals, tobacco tins, rugby jerseys, commemorative stamps, coins, bank notes, and much more besides. The dog has become a kind of visual shorthand for the entire island, and one that is accepted by all Irish traditions. When Van Morrison released *Veedon Fleece*, and its cover showed him sitting beside two Wolfhounds, the theme of his album could only be Ireland.

There is also something about this breed of dog that seems to inspire a degree of unbridled romantic fantasy. Edward Jesse, a Wolfhound enthusiast, speculated that:

> when princely hospitality was to be found in the old palaces, castles, and baronial halls of fair Erin, it is hardly possible to imagine anything more aristocratic and imposing than the aspect of these dogs, while attending the banquets of their masters.

In November 2012, the Irish Kennel Club asked the Irish government to provide protection to the country's native dog breeds, with a request that special attention be given to the Irish Wolfhound. In its submission to the government, the club stated that this breed had been 'kept by the Irish for centuries', that it was 'a symbol of our national heritage', and that its origins 'stretch back into the mists of Irish time'.

There is a very strong case for recognising the Wolfhound as a symbol of national heritage. Indeed, that is how it is already viewed in many parts of the world. It could also be argued that this symbol has its roots in the distant mists of Irish time. However, the origins of the contemporary Wolfhound lie a good deal closer to home. In reality, the dog, as it exists today, is the product of a breeding programme that began in the 1860s on an estate in rural Gloucestershire, and was directed by a wealthy English gentleman who used a number of Russian, Scottish, English and Tibetan animals to help produce what is now regarded as the quintessential Irish dog.

Once again, the question might be posed: does that matter? For some, it seems to matter a great deal. Michael

Brandow believes that the 'resuscitation' of the 'so-called Irish Wolfhound' in the nineteenth century can only have been truly miraculous—because the breed was already extinct. He clearly regards the claims made by breeders for the dog's ancient lineage as either self-delusional or as a marketing ploy. I agree with him that modern Wolfhounds may have very little of their namesakes' bloodlines, but I would also argue that, over time, they have become Irish—by adoption, if not by blood.

For me, the Wolfhound was a creature that I first encountered in the realm of fiction, and I can recall my feelings when, as a child, I met a living specimen of the breed for the first time. Of course, I felt overwhelmed by the tremendous size of the animal, but there were other qualities that also struck me. It was the grace, the gentleness and the dignity with which the dog carried itself that impressed me most. Those are virtues that I am happy to see associated with Ireland. If this breed might be considered as a 'mongrel', or even as a kind of fiction in itself, then so much the better. 'What race,' James Joyce wrote in 1907, 'can boast of being pure today?' He went on to suggest that 'no race has less right to utter such a boast than the race now living in Ireland'.

Throughout much of the nineteenth century, the Wolfhound served as an emblem for the noblest aspirations of the Irish people, and his likeness was carved on tombs and public monuments, both in Ireland and in many places where Irish emigrants had settled. Wolfhounds can be found on the memorial in St Patrick's Church of Ireland Cathedral in Dublin to commemorate those Irish soldiers who fought and died in Britain's colonial wars, but they also appear on the monument to Daniel O'Connell, the 'Liberator' of Catholic Ireland, in the city centre, and on the one that was raised at Gettysburg to mark the role that Irish soldiers played in that battle.

When Ireland's President Michael D. Higgins paid a historic visit to the UK in 2012, he was greeted at Windsor Castle by the British Royal family, and by Domhnail, the Wolfhound who is the current mascot of the Irish Guards. During the commemorations designed to mark the centenary of the Irish Rebellion of 1916, Wolfhounds also featured prominently as part of the official celebrations. Over the past two centuries there have been, to say the least, few other icons able to transcend the religious and political differences that have caused so much historic division in Ireland.

The Wolfhound proved able to fulfil that symbolic role for much of the nineteenth century. However, in the early years of the following one, an unlikely contender for the role of Ireland's national dog emerged. The champions of that animal did not pretend that it could claim an ancient lineage in Ireland to compare with the Wolfhound—in fact, the founding sire of this breed was not even supposed to have been Irish.

Rebellion: the Kerry Blue Terrier

The terrier that we now call the Kerry Blue may seem, at first, to have little in common with the dignified and graceful Wolfhound. The ancestors of the humble terrier did not, after all, spend much time in the company of feudal chiefs, princes or kings. They did not lie at their lords' feet during royal banquets, or take part in the ritual of any court's hunting expeditions. Their presence was not sought out by foreign potentates or diplomats, and they were seldom required to pose for portraits with their masters. The heroic deeds of the Irish Wolfhound are chronicled in the ancient Celtic sagas, but there are few references to the Blue Terrier before the twentieth century. The Wolfhound chased and killed ferocious wolves; the Kerry Blue was a rat-catcher.

Nonetheless, the Wolfhound and the Blue Terrier are connected in some unexpected ways, and despite their differences they both came to represent a concept of Ireland— though in different ways, and to different groups of Irish men and women. They also share a propensity to attract romantic myths and legends. In the case of the terrier these usually involve stories in which an exotic blue dog swims ashore from a ship that has foundered in Tralee Bay in County Kerry. At times this is said to be a Spanish galleon, part of the great Armada, struggling to make its way home in heavy seas. In other accounts the ship is a Russian schooner that went down with all hands. Sometimes it is only a modest Portuguese fishing boat. In all of these stories, the dog that managed to reach the shore soon hooked up with some of the local bitches. Indeed, according to some accounts, he mated with every bitch in Kerry, and the result of his numerous romantic liaisons was the Blue Terrier.

Sadly, none of these legends seems to have any basis in reality. Dogs were seldom kept on board sailing ships, and when they were they were more likely to be water dogs (which could retrieve lines lost overboard or carry messages between ships) and not terriers, a breed that likes to keep its paws firmly planted on dry land. Indeed, the roots of the term 'terrier' are believed to lie in the Latin word 'terram' meaning 'ground'. In any case, the Kerry Blue is clearly related to other Irish terriers such as the Wheaten, from whom the blue dog is probably descended.

It seems likely that all the different types of native Irish terrier share some common ancestors, and their breeds only became distinct through a range of variable local factors, which were sometimes heightened through deliberate breeding programmes. Whatever the claims made about this terrier's precise beginnings, most Kerry Blue loyalists are convinced of an underlying truth: in the words of Dr E. S. Montgomery, an authority on terrier breeds, the dog is:

> a true and distinct breed indigenous to Ireland and, though no man can trace accurately its origin, all men will admit its antiquity.

The first probable reference to the Kerry Blue comes from 1847, when Major Richardson, the Wolfhound breeder and enthusiast, described what he termed 'a harlequin terrier'. There have been some who question that the Kerry dog can genuinely be described as blue. However, Richardson reported that the dog was 'a blueish slate-colour, marked with darker blotches and patches'. He also observed that the terrier was 'one of the most determined of its race': an assessment that might also suggest he was referring to the Kerry dog, which had a reputation for toughness and aggression. Indeed, according to one enthusiast, no one in Ireland would raise a Kerry Blue unless the dog was found to be 'dead game', and those with 'the yellow streak' were given 'short shrift', and soon disposed of by their owners. If true, it suggests that a robust approach to the culling of substandard dogs was not confined to the Irish gentry.

The Kerry Blues were reputed to be the only dogs capable of killing an otter 'single-handed, and in deep water', and their use in otter hunts continued into the twentieth century. They were also said to be adept and 'game' at fighting badgers. One show judge wrote:

> There is no doubt, [if a terrier] goes down into the
> bowels of the earth in perfect darkness and [meets]
> a big fighting badger entrenched there, he must be
> game.

It seems that these terriers were often used for dog fights in the nineteenth century, and this practice also appears to have persisted well into the twentieth. The breed's instinct to chase vermin and small animals was encouraged for much of that period. Indeed, in early Irish dog shows, the Kerry Blues were required to pass 'gameness' tests, which included their ability to chase, catch and kill live rabbits. Their enthusiasm for this activity is said to have earned them the nickname of the 'Blue Devils'.

Although Richardson described the terrier as 'a recognised variety of extreme beauty', he did not mention County Kerry in his description of this blue dog. Terriers of a similar colour had developed in other Irish counties such as Wicklow and Tipperary, and until relatively recently blue pups would appear from time to time in the litters thrown by Wheaten and Irish Terriers. When the first club for the breed was formed in 1919 it was called the Irish Blue Terriers Club, and it was not until the 1920s that the name of Kerry Blue was widely adopted. Given the popularity of the breed with Irish Nationalists, it may seem ironic that the dog was first called the 'Kerry Blue' in England—where it had been introduced by Lord Kenmare, an extensive landowner in County Kerry.

Irish farmers may have chosen to keep a medium-sized terrier like the Kerry dog because only substantial landowners were once permitted to keep large hunting dogs, and their tenants were restricted to smaller dogs that were incapable of killing big animals, such as deer. Kerry Blues were reputed to be used frequently for poaching, and there seems little doubt that this breed would have made an excellent accomplice for any poachers hoping to help themselves to some of their landlord's game. Perhaps this hint of the Kerry Blue's rebellious character also contributed to the subsequent appeal that the animal held for a generation of Irish revolutionaries.

Once again, however, the truth seems to be more prosaic. Originally, the Blue Terrier was less of a pet than a working farm dog, with all of the everyday chores and activities which that entailed. An idea of just what this work meant was provided by a farmer who kept some Kerry Blues in the 1920s:

> In the morning they herd the cattle; at noon they come in and tread the wheel to churn the butter; in the afternoon they herd again; and after supper they are turned out to guard the sheep, the chickens and geese and the pigs.

The Blue would also have been expected to catch any vermin on the farm. In the context of this relentless work schedule, the Blue Terrier did not have the opportunity to acquire the airs and graces of some more pampered breeds, and this may further explain the dog's appeal to the democratic ideology of radical Irish Nationalists, who tended to view the over-indulgence of some domestic pets in moralistic terms, and even as evidence of the creeping 'anglicisation' of their country.

Kerry Blue Terriers did not make their first appearance in an Irish dog show until 1913. The show was in Cork, and there were just five entries. According to one spectator, there was considerable variation in the size and appearance of the dogs competing in their class. Frank Butler was one of the judges at a show in Killarney a few years later, when there were twenty entries. It was, he wrote, 'a sight I had never seen before, and I do not suppose I shall ever see again'. He noted that the exhibits were 'of all sizes', ranging from 'a small fox terrier to an Old English Sheepdog'. Butler believed that most of the terriers were kept 'for fighting purposes', and he claimed that it proved hard to keep any kind of order between them, with some of the owners being 'nearly as bad as the dogs'.

A photo dating from this show reveals little similarity to the breed that is now called the Kerry Blue. This is partly a question of presentation: the terrier in the photo, who finished third in his class, looks shaggy and lacks obvious signs of trimming or any other form of grooming. But this is not just a matter of cosmetics: the Kerry Blue, as photographed in 1916, seems to display few of the characteristic features of the modern dog. Looking at this picture, it is hard to believe the changes that were about to take place, or the great surge in popularity that this breed of dog was about to experience.

In the early years of the twentieth century, the Blue Terrier began to be identified as a sort of 'people's dog' by some Irish Nationalists. Unlike the Wolfhound (and many of its owners), the Blue had an actual job. The dog's status as a working animal, its combative nature, the evident lack of social pretension on the part of its typical owners, and the sense of sturdy independence the Kerry Blue conveyed, all combined to appeal to many of those who considered themselves 'nationally minded', and who perhaps believed that they shared the same qualities as the Kerry Blue dog.

There were other compelling reasons why this dog was favoured by radical Nationalists. All of the larger breeds that were native to Ireland—the Wolfhounds, Red Setters, Red and White Setters and Water Spaniels—were connected, to a greater or lesser extent, with the landed gentry, and therefore with Unionist politics. The Glen of Imaal Terrier certainly did not have that connection. However, as a dwarf breed, it may not have had sufficient stature—both in figurative and in literal terms—to represent an independent Irish nation. It was also virtually unknown even within Ireland, and its probable origins did not lie in a proud Celtic past, but in the more recent history of English colonisation. The Soft-Coated Wheaten was not yet recognised by any Kennel Club as a distinct purebred, or even as a separate breed. Neither was the Kerry Beagle, which was also associated with fox hunting, the archetypal pastime of the Irish gentry. The Irish Terrier had been developed as a breed in the heart of Unionist Ulster. It may also have seemed compromised in the eyes of radical Nationalists by its connection with English royalty, as well as by the high-profile and active role the dog had played during World War One in regiments of the British Army.

That left the Kerry Blue as the only native breed with sufficient credentials of appearance and pedigree to be considered as Ireland's alternative National Dog. The fact that its founding sire was supposed to have been Spanish, Russian or Portuguese was discreetly ignored.

In its own way, the growth of popularity of the Kerry Blue in the early years of the twentieth century mirrored the growth of other 'Irish-Ireland' activities, such as learning the Irish language, playing Gaelic games or wearing what were fondly considered to be Ireland's ancient national costumes. Blue Terriers appealed to Nationalists because of their background, which seemed to fit Douglas Hyde's criteria for 'de-anglicising' Ireland: these dogs were 'racy, of the soil', and above all 'Irish'. No doubt, radical Nationalists also welcomed the recognition that the Kerry Blue soon received outside Ireland. However, once the dog had been recognised as a distinct breed in the UK and the United States, the process of selective breeding and grooming began in earnest. The setting-up of Blue Terrier clubs in Great Britain and America in the early years of the twentieth century also led to greater conformity, and helped to establish breed standards and points of merit. Before long, the Kerry Blue began to take on the appearance that we can now recognise in the contemporary show dog. It is, once again, somewhat ironic that the current stylised features of this Irish breed were largely developed outside Ireland.

When the first Blue Terrier Club was formed in Dublin, Ireland was caught up in the turbulent aftermath of the 1916 Easter Rising, and was convulsed by the War of Independence. The new club quickly became a convenient meeting place for young radical Nationalists, and the Blue Terrier emerged as a sort of mascot for them. There were soon a number of clubs in Dublin promoting the interests of the breed, and the legality of staging dog shows in Ireland had become another issue on which the British administration could be confronted.

In 1920, all dog shows in Ireland were obliged to be held under a licence granted by the Kennel Club in England, which styled itself as 'the' Kennel Club. However, on 16 October of that year, the Dublin Blue Terrier Club held a breed show in the north-Dublin suburb of Summerhill in open defiance of that regulation. One of the club's members was a young man called Michael Collins. He may have been a devotee of Kerry Blues, but Collins also had a wide range of other consuming interests. He was a member of the Irish parliament (Dáil Éireann); the Minister for Finance in the provisional Irish government; the Director of Organisation and Arms Procurement for the Irish Republican Army; and the President of the Irish Republican Brotherhood. In 1920, Collins was leading the IRA's military campaign against the British presence in Ireland, and Dublin Castle, the centre of the British administration, had offered a reward of £10,000 for any information leading to his capture or death.

Although Collins and many other like-minded individuals had been attracted to the Blue Terrier Club, its membership was not wholly confined to radical Nationalists. In fact, a number of well-known Unionists and leading figures in the British administration in Ireland had also joined. One of these was the serving Under-Secretary of State, Sir James McMahon. Part of his duties involved sending and receiving coded messages from London. This was in the middle of an intense guerrilla war being waged against the British presence in Ireland, so the exchange of confidential messages between London and Dublin was of considerable importance. McMahon had appointed a young woman to handle this highly sensitive coding operation, blissfully unaware that she was a cousin of Michael Collins, and immediately passed any useful information on to him.

Another member of the Blue Terrier Club was Captain the Honourable Valentine Maurice Wyndham-Quin, the younger son of the Earl of Dunraven. When he joined the Terrier Club, Wyndham-Quin was serving as a military attaché to the Lord Lieutenant of Ireland in the vice-regal lodge in Dublin's Phoenix Park. It may seem remarkable that men whose political opinions were so fundamentally (and violently) opposed as Collins and Wyndham-Quin were members of the same club. Indeed, when I wrote an article about this for an Irish newspaper some years ago, I received a number of letters from people who were outraged at the suggestion that they might have enjoyed friendly personal relations.

Some also claimed that Collins was much too busy running a guerrilla war to have owned a Kerry Blue, let alone to have socialised with officials of the British Empire at a mere dog show. In fact, Collins's attendance at the show is not so improbable as it may initially seem. When the British were searching for him all over Ireland, Collins adopted the bold strategy of 'hiding in plain view'. According to the historian T. Ryle Dwyer, he delighted in moving freely around Ireland with apparent recklessness. He believed, correctly, that the air of careless normality he assumed was his best and most effective disguise.

The Irish Kennel Club records that Michael Collins was the eighteenth person to register a dog with the Dublin Blue Terrier Club. He may even have known the Wyndham-Quins, who had already donated a trophy for outstanding terriers (which is still being competed for nowadays). According to Tim Pat Coogan, Collins was in the habit of giving unexpected presents of Kerry Blue pups to many of his friends, including some of those who would later take the opposing side to Collins in Ireland's bitter civil war. Collins later donated a trophy to the Terrier Club, the Mícheál Ó Coileáin Perpetual Cup (which is also still competed for).

The Blue Terrier Club's first show was held on a Saturday evening in October 1920, when an after-dark curfew was operating throughout Dublin. The curfew was an attempt to curb the activities of Collins and the IRA. According to one account, those who attended the event 'risked arrest or even death'. Nonetheless, it seems that Collins was still able to enter a dog for the Wyndham-Quin trophy. The name of his Kerry Blue, 'Convict 224', gave some indication of the political sympathies of its owner. That was the prison number given to Éamon de Valera (a man who was then Collins's ally, but would soon become his bitterest foe) when he was in jail in Wales. The names of some other entries included 'Dawn of Freedom' and 'Markiewicz', but there were also some names that might indicate Unionist sympathies, such as the 'Munster Fusilier', named after a British Army regiment. Collins's dog did not win the competition, but the young captain from the vice-regal lodge did present the winner's cup. He may have been unaware that one of the judges of the terrier contest was also a leading member of the IRA.

The following month saw a major escalation of political violence in Ireland, and a turning point in the island's modern history. On the morning of Sunday 21 November 1920, fourteen suspected agents of British Intelligence were assassinated in Dublin on the direct orders of Collins. Later that afternoon, the Auxiliary Division of the Royal Irish Constabulary opened fire on a crowd attending a Gaelic football match and killed fourteen civilians. Violence continued to rage in the months that followed, before both sides agreed to a truce in July 1921. A subsequent peace conference led to the Anglo–Irish Treaty in December of that year, which ended British rule in the twenty-six counties of Ireland that became known as Saorstat Éireann—the Irish Free State.

When Michael Collins signed the Treaty on behalf of the Irish provisional government, he had predicted that he was signing his own death warrant, and that proved to be the case. In June of 1922 a civil war broke out in Ireland between those who accepted the terms of the Anglo–Irish Treaty and those who opposed them. Collins became commander-in-chief of Ireland's new National Army, and prosecuted the civil war against his former comrades with his customary zeal and vigour. But that did not mean he had forgotten the Kerry Blue Terrier. In fact, towards the end of 1922, he was drawing up plans for Dáil Éireann officially to recognise the Kerry Blue as Ireland's National Dog. Sadly, before these plans, or any others, could be realised, Michael Collins was assassinated in an ambush at the Béal na Bláth crossroads in County Cork. In the years that immediately followed his death, the Kerry Blue did achieve the popular, if not the official, recognition in Ireland that he had wished. However, it could be argued that the breed was later to prove a victim of its own success.

Counter-Revolution

The Kerry Blue Terrier became something of a romantic symbol among young Irish men in the 1920s, and its popularity dramatically increased throughout the country. According to D. J. Smyth, an early member of the Irish Kennel Club, many young men in Dublin were once accompanied by their bull terriers:

> you'd see them at football matches, and they'd always have a dog [...] they didn't go in for badger baiting, more for dog fights.

When it became known that Michael Collins, the great hero of the War of Independence, favoured the Blue Terrier, 'those chaps who used to be with bull terriers changed over to the Kerry Blue'.

The growing popularity of the breed was not confined to Ireland. Kerry Blues were first exhibited in England at Crufts in 1922—the year of Collins's death. When the dog first appeared in the American Westminster show in the early 1920s it was entered as a 'Blue Black Terrier', and was shown untrimmed and in a 'Miscellaneous' class. In 1925 a Kerry Blue club was formed in the plush surroundings of the Waldorf–Astoria Hotel in New York, and the breed was formally recognised by the American Kennel Club within a few months of its foundation.

The founders of the American club decided to follow the breed standard that had been written by the English Kerry Blue club rather than the Irish one. 'Although Ireland is entitled to the credit for developing the breed,' wrote one American historian of the Kerry Blue, 'the English contributed greatly to the refinement of the [dog] and to its excellence in the show ring.' It was believed that the 'wide experience' and 'constructive breeding methods' of the English terrier breeders were superior to those of the Irish, and so 'the English Standard was followed in all major categories in preference to the Irish'. No doubt Michael Collins turned in his grave.

Following the success of the 1920 Blue Terrier event in Dublin, it was decided to stage a further show that would be open on this occasion to all other breeds. It was planned that the exhibition would take place on St Patrick's Day 1921, in the Concert Rooms on Dublin's North Brunswick Street. By far the largest number of breed entries was in the Kerry Blue class, with more than 250 dogs being shown. This show has been described as 'the ultimate act of defiance' on two counts. It was held, once again, in explicit rejection of the legal obligation to obtain a license from the British Kennel Club. Beyond that, it also challenged the British Club's tradition of staging its own show in Dublin on St Patrick's Day. In 1921 the British show still took place in Dublin's affluent Merrion Square, but it seems to have been a very damp squib in comparison with the other event.

That was the last time that the British Kennel Club organised an exhibition in Ireland. The first Irish show had been staged by the Terrier Club, but this acted as a kind of catalyst, and the following year the Dublin Blue Terrier Club reconstituted itself as the Irish Kennel Club. It seems fitting that the first dog to be registered with the new club was a Kerry Blue.

Despite its early connection with radical Irish Nationalism, the Irish Kennel Club reached across Ireland's political and sectarian divisions from its inception. The first chairman of the club was Justice Henry Hanna—not only a committed Unionist, but an Ulster Presbyterian to boot. He is said to have fashioned a 'motley assortment of well-meaning but inexperienced dog fanciers' into a coherent and well-organised group. Hanna expressed the hope that their example might encourage other Irishmen to realise what could be achieved 'with honest endeavour and goodwill' if they were prepared to 'join hands in a united effort'. A succeeding president, Henry Fottrell, described Hanna's contribution to dog-breeding in Ireland as 'incalculable'.

The Irish Kennel Club was established just as Ireland was being partitioned into two separate states, and it did not operate on an all-Ireland basis. However, its membership crossed some of the existing divisions in Irish society, and this non-sectarian tradition has been maintained in subsequent years. Civil society in Northern Ireland tends to be polarised along historic denominational lines, and in the past centuries those underlying divisions have periodically erupted in communal conflict and political violence.

On one occasion, the dog-breeding community in Northern Ireland felt the impact of such sectarian aggression. In 1978 the IRA firebombed the La Mon restaurant near

Belfast. The Irish Collie Club was holding its annual dinner dance in the hotel that night, and took the full force of the explosion. Twelve people were burned to death, including a school friend of mine and his wife.

Thankfully, that was an exceptional occurrence. Nowadays, both the British and Irish Kennel Clubs stage shows in Northern Ireland, but these are not held in competition with each other. According to Sean Delmar, president of the Irish Kennel Club, around one third of owners registering dogs with the Irish Kennel Club live in Northern Ireland: I can vouch that northern accents are frequently heard at dog shows in the Republic, and the reverse is also the case. The biggest dog show of the year, run by the Irish Kennel Club, has taken place every St Patrick's Day since 1921, and attracts visitors from all over the island. For many years it was staged in the fashionable grounds of the Royal Dublin Society in the affluent suburb of Ballsbridge, and was regarded as something of an institution—though not always for the more obvious or predictable reasons.

In the first decade of the twentieth century, James O'Mara, an Irish Nationalist MP at Westminster, had grown concerned by the amount of alcohol that was consumed in Ireland on St Patrick's Day, particularly since it occurred during Lent. He introduced a bill to the House of Commons that made it compulsory for all public houses in Ireland to close on 17 March. O'Mara was supported in the British House of Lords by the Earl of Dunraven (Captain Wyndham-Quin's father), and his bill was passed. This legislation was not repealed until the early 1970s, and it meant that for most of the twentieth century it was illegal to buy alcohol in Ireland on St Patrick's Day. However, certain exceptions were made, and alcoholic drink could be served to bona fide members of the Irish Kennel Club on the day of its annual show.

As a consequence, the club could expect an influx of new members in March of every year, many of whom had displayed no previous interest in dogs or dog shows, but were known to be fond of drink. According to urban legend, the playwright Brendan Behan was in the habit of gathering up any stray mutt he could find and using it to blag his way into the members' lounge of the annual dog show. The poet Patrick Kavanagh was also alleged to have paid a young woman for the 'rent' of her dog on that one day every year.

One genuine owner of purebred Kerry Blue Terriers in the 1920s was May Beckett (the mother of the Nobel Laureate Samuel Beckett). The Becketts lived in the well-off district of Foxrock in south County Dublin, which was then considered to be something of a Protestant and Unionist enclave. May Beckett is generally considered to have been an emotionally withdrawn woman who lavished an open affection on her dogs that she denied to her younger son. Samuel Beckett sometimes has the reputation of being a cerebral and austere intellectual. It is true that he was not in the habit of wearing his heart on his sleeve, but, for me, his work expresses the most profound of human values and emotions. He also shared his mother's feelings of deep affection for the family dogs, and spent long hours walking the Wicklow hills accompanied by a Kerry Blue.

Beckett was particularly fond of one of the terriers, a bitch called Wolf. In time, the beloved dog grew old and sick, and Beckett's mother arranged for her to be euthanised while Beckett was away from home. 'The old bitch was destroyed,' Beckett wrote, 'unbeknownst to me.' He was extremely upset, and said he had 'wanted to be with [Wolf] at the end, to try and make it perhaps a little easier'. His mother apparently thought the dog should be put down, or 'destroyed' in Sam's words, in his absence to spare him the pain of seeing her die. However, Beckett found he 'could not take a reasonable view' of the terrier's death, and became so depressed that it has been claimed he contemplated suicide.

Dogs feature with surprising regularity in his subsequent novels and plays. Beckett writes about them with considerable empathy, but does not claim to understand what he regards as the unknowable nature of a foreign species. In his early novel *Malone Dies*, he describes an old dog that is fast approaching death. Beckett being Beckett, this is written with the underlying emotion working against the grain of obvious sentimentality, and the passage carries a characteristic sting of black humour in its tail:

> To old dogs the hour comes when, whistled by their master setting forth with his stick at dawn, they cannot spring after him. Then they stay in their kennel, or in their basket, though they are not chained, and listen to the steps dying away. The man too is sad. But soon the pure air and the sun console him, he thinks no more about his old companion until evening. The lights in his house bid him welcome home and a feeble barking makes him say, It is time I had him destroyed.

The Kerry Blue may have once appealed to those who viewed the terrier as being, in some respects, at the opposite end of the social and political spectrum to the Irish Wolfhound. But some believe that the two have a blood connection, and that the Blue Terrier may even claim the ancient Wolfhound as one of its ancestors. An article in the *Stock Keeper*, for example, proposed that Irish Terriers as they 'existed in the Emerald Isle before the cunning hand of the exhibitor had been run over [them] were the descendants of the Wolfhound'. That might sound too far-fetched to be credible, but what may seem like incompatible breeds have been known to mate, so the notion of these two having offspring is not out of the question.

The similarity of appearance between three-week-old Wolfhound puppies with three-month-old Kerry Blues has been cited as proof of 'a consanguinity that cannot be doubted'. That seems a dubious argument to me, but some enthusiasts of the Kerry Blue breed have gone even further, and have argued that the claim of their dogs to be genuine descendants of 'the old Wolfhound' are stronger than 'the modern product', which only originated with Captain Graham. I suppose it is not impossible.

Throughout the 1920s, one in every four pups registered with the Irish Kennel Club was a Kerry Blue. But while the popularity of the Wolfhound has increased in recent years, the following that the Kerry Blue enjoyed in the first half of the last century has diminished with the passage of time. Some have noticed that its eclipse has coincided with the growth in popularity of the Miniature Schnauzer—a breed that strongly resembles the Kerry Blue, but which is, as its name suggests, a good deal smaller and rather easier to maintain.

There may be some truth in that claim, but in reality most breeds of terrier have experienced a comparable decline throughout the world in recent years, and there are no doubt many other contributing reasons. In the case of Ireland, there could be a number of specific factors at work. Perhaps the popularity of the breed among Irish Nationalists faded along with some of their hopes of what the new Irish state might deliver to its citizens. George Bernard Shaw offered one bleak assessment of the highly conservative and theocentric state that emerged from the fight for Irish independence:

> Under the feeble and apologetic tyranny of [the British], we Irish were forced to endure a considerable degree of compulsory freedom. The moment we got rid of that tyranny, we rushed to enslave ourselves.

Perhaps it would be fairer to suggest that other dreams simply took the place of those held by the founders of the Irish state. As Ireland gained in material prosperity, and took its place among other thoroughly modern nations in the European Union, the charm of a 'people's dog' that herded cattle, guarded pigs and hunted rabbits may have lessened in the eyes of an upwardly mobile population.

There are, of course, other explanations that can help to account for the fall in numbers of the Kerry Blue, which has made its future uncertain. It is now vulnerable to extinction, even in its own country. But, sadly, the Kerry Blue Terrier is not the only one of Ireland's native breeds whose popularity has declined in the course of the past century. In one case, the decline in the breed's acceptance cannot be attributed to changing political or social circumstances. The popularity of this dog was not only eclipsed by its close blood relative, but by a breed that it had helped to create.

The Original: the Irish Red and White Setter

There may be two widespread misconceptions about the Irish Red and White Setter. Its name might suggest that this setter is essentially a red dog with white markings. It may also imply that the Red and White Setter is derived from the Red Setter, and represents in some way a dilution of the purity of the all-red breed. In reality, the Red and White Setter is a white dog with red markings, and is almost certainly the predecessor and ancestor of the current Red Setter. Indeed, one of the best-known early examples of the all-red breed, William Hutchinson's 'Bob', is said to have been a direct descendant of a famous line of Red and Whites that was bred in the early nineteenth century. There are obvious similarities in appearance, use and temperament between the Red and White and its better-known and more popular cousin, but there are also some important distinctions, and their recent histories are very different.

It seems likely that Irish Setters were developed out of various breeds of spaniel, and there is certainly a passing resemblance between the Brittany Spaniel and the Red and White Setter. A distinctive breed of setter seems to have emerged in Ireland in the course of the eighteenth century. According to Colonel

J. K. Milner, an early historian of Irish Setters, this coincided with the period 'from the time of the immortal King William to the unfortunate uprising of 1798', when 'Irishmen had nothing to interfere with their sporting pursuits'. According to Milner, Ireland was then 'the fairest land in the civilized world for manly sport'. It was certainly something of a golden age for members of Ireland's landed gentry like Colonel Milner, but those who experienced the recurrent famines of that century, or who suffered under the oppressive Penal Laws, are likely to have disagreed with his assessment that everyone in Ireland, 'rich and poor', was caught up in the same 'rollicking love of sport' as the good Colonel (who won a gold medal for shooting in the 1908 Olympics).

In fact, some types of setter may have appeared in Ireland long before the eighteenth century, and before the widespread introduction of guns. The original purpose of the dog was to hunt game birds such as partridge, grouse and snipe. When the dog has located the bird, he would 'set'—with one foreleg raised, and with his muzzle pointed in the bird's direction. According to the sixteenth-century naturalist John Keys (who was better known by the Latin form of his name, Johannes Caius), the dog would then creep forward 'like a worme' until the hunter had reached 'the place of the byrde's last abode', and then a net would be thrown over the quarry. Once firearms became more generally available, from the late seventeenth century, setters began to be developed into proper gun dogs. Their role was still to point towards the location of the game by scenting the air, and they still flushed out the birds, but now they also had to remain motionless after the game had risen to avoid distracting the hunter—as well as to lessen the risk of being shot. The refusal to chase goes against the instinct of most dogs, and requires firm discipline and training.

The shooting of game proved a popular pastime for Ireland's landed gentry. According to Dr Albrecht Ua Siaghail, a Red and White Setter breeder, the dogs they used may have been 'owned by the anglo ascendancy', but they were 'cared for by the disinherited Irish'. According to the same writer, these dogs roamed 'the green fields and uplands of the Gael', and were dependent for their food and sustenance on the 'hapless native population', even during the 'ignominious famine period'. To say the least, this interpretation of Ireland's canine history seems fanciful, and reminiscent of one of Boucicault's more lurid melodramas. There is ample evidence that Ireland's landowning classes were devoted to their dogs (perhaps excessively so), and the carefully tended pet cemeteries that were frequently found on their estates are testimony to that devotion. The notion that starving tenants would feed their landlords' dogs before themselves or their families, however, seems far-fetched to me.

Well-trained and skilful hunting dogs could be very valuable in monetary terms. Writing in 1848, William Youatt mentioned that a 'true Irish Setter' would obtain a higher price 'than an English or Scotch one'. He quotes a figure of 200 guineas (a huge sum in today's money) 'for a brace of them'. In that context it is absurd to think that these pedigree animals would have been so neglected by their owners that they risked starving to death. Indeed, the sad truth is that some landlords would rather have seen their tenants starve than their dogs.

Unlike their English counterparts, the Irish gentry proved more partial to setters than pointers. According to one contemporary account, this was because setters were better adapted to the Irish landscape. They could cover 'more ground than pointers', were 'not so liable to get footsore', and could 'bear the change of weather better than the latter'. Over time, a setter was developed that was unique to Ireland. Paintings and prints from the eighteenth and early nineteenth centuries show a hunting dog that looks very similar to the current Red and White Setter in colour, shape and size. By then there were several varieties of setter to be found in different regions of Ireland. Given the practical difficulties that travel within Ireland could involve at that time, it is not surprising that different varieties of the breed developed in different parts of the country. Although the majority of these were red and white, there were also some that were pure white, and some that were solid red. Some carried what became known as the 'shower of hail'—a band of small dark red markings across a white muzzle or flank that resemble human freckles.

For many years, red and white dogs were believed to be hardier than their red relatives. It was also easier to see them against the dark heather and bog background of the Irish countryside. In fact, hunters were said sometimes to tie white handkerchiefs around Red Setters' necks to make them stand out against the landscape. All of these dogs—red, white, and red and white—were defined as 'Irish Setters', and were generally regarded as belonging to the same breed. Considerable interbreeding between the different colours is likely to have occurred, and when all-red dogs were bred with other all-red specimens, they could still produce setters with white markings. It was not until the nineteenth century that the appearance of sporting dogs began to be given as much consideration as their abilities in the field, and colour became an issue of vital importance to breeders. From that point, the all-red setter began to grow rapidly in popularity, and in numbers.

In 1873, the two types of setters were exhibited in the same class at Dublin's Rotunda Gardens show. There seems to have been a good number of Red and White Setters taking part, but this may be regarded as a turning point, and the beginning of a decline in the numbers and popularity of the original setter. According to one Red and White Setter owner, it was the 'flashiness' of the all-red dog that appealed both to the judges and the public, not only on the day of the Rotunda show, but 'from that time forward'. With remarkable speed, the demand for Red Setters grew, and that was reflected in the high prices that good specimens could fetch.

Before long, in the words of one critic, the solid red dog had 'taken the world by storm'. In a parallel development, the popularity of the original Irish Setter went into a rapid decline. In 1875 there were sixty-six entries in the Irish Setter class at a conformation show in Dublin, and forty-three of them were red. The following year at a show in Cork, there were ninety-six entries, and sixty of those were also all-red dogs. This imbalance grew even more pronounced in the closing years of the nineteenth century, and it soon became unusual even to see a Red and White Setter in the show ring.

It has been claimed that the decline of the original Irish Setter coincided with the 'repatriation' of Irish landlords to England (following the legislative reforms enacted at Westminster that divested the Irish gentry of much of their land), and that the Red and White Setters only managed to find 'a tenuous line of survival' due to the 'furtive breeding of the stock' by Ireland's 'native population'. Once again, this interpretation seems fanciful. It is true that the Irish gentry lost most of their political, economic and social influence in the course of the nineteenth century. It is also true that many landowners were compelled to sell their estates through the special courts that had been established for that purpose by the British government. In that sense, any references to the 'Ascendancy' had already become anachronistic. As Hubert Butler once observed, by this stage the landlord class could more accurately be termed the 'Descendancy'. In any case, the bulk of Irish landlords could not have been 'repatriated' to England since Ireland had long since become their home. Purebred Red and White Setters were still kept in some of the remaining estates belonging to the Irish gentry, such as that owned by the Rossmore family in Monaghan, who maintained the Red and White Setter breed for more than 200 years. However, it was not until the 1920s that concerted attempts to preserve the breed were made.

A crucial role in preserving the original setter was played by a Presbyterian minister in the north of Ireland. Noble Huston was born in the small village of Ballyscullion in the heart of rural Ulster in 1868. His family had kept Red and White Setters in his youth, and he had become aware that the breed was in serious decline. In 1908 Huston became Minister of the First Presbyterian Church in Ballynahinch in County Down—a position he would hold for the next thirty-seven years. This was one of the oldest Presbyterian congregations in Ireland, dating back to the early seventeenth century.

Huston lived across the road from the local Catholic parish priest. Apparently, the priest kept dairy cattle, while Huston kept bees as well as breeding dogs. It was said that, together, they could have created a land of milk and honey.

Huston served as a chaplain to the 36th (Ulster) Division during World War One, and witnessed the heavy casualties that it suffered when half of its numbers were killed or wounded during the first two days of the Somme offensive. The war had brought hardship not only to Irish troops and the people of Ireland, but also to Irish dogs. There had been a general shortage of food, and the breeding of animals for sport had become almost non-existent. As a result, the number of Irish Setters had fallen. In 1914, 164 all-red setters had been registered with the Kennel Club; by 1919 only a third of that number remained. This decline was even more marked with the Red and White Setter, and that breed seemed on the verge of extinction in the war's aftermath.

Huston set about breeding Red and Whites with a strong sense of urgency and purpose. He was adamant that his goal was not to create a new breed, and certainly not to produce what he called 'a revived breed like the Irish Wolfhound', but merely to assist what he termed a 'continued breed'. As part of that goal, he began to record Red and White Setter pedigrees, some of which he was able to trace back to the eighteenth century.

Along with his cousin Dr Elliot from County Monaghan, Huston also embarked on an intensive breeding programme that drew upon any purebred Red and White Setters they were able to locate. The first pair of these came from Monaghan: a setter bitch called Gyp, which Huston bred with Glen, a Red and White Setter he had acquired from the Rossmore family. Subsequently, Gyp was mated with another setter called Johnny. These three dogs are considered to have provided the foundation stock for the modern Red and White Setter.

Huston believed that the way in which pedigree dogs, and Red Setters in particular, had become commercialised in recent years had damaged vulnerable breeds like the Red and White Setters, and he deplored the impact of what he called the 'deleterious show ring'. It is hard not to feel some sympathy with his dismay at the emphasis that the growth of dog shows had placed upon physical appearance. The Red Setters that appeared in exhibitions had developed longer coats and more luxuriant feathering on their legs and tails, which may have added to their allure, but would have proved rather impractical in the field. This sort of development was, in Huston's view, at the expense of more important qualities such as courage, endurance and character.

It is tempting to detect evidence of an underlying Presbyterian suspicion of the 'flashy' glamour and worldly appeal of the all-red breed, and it is not surprising that Huston placed a great deal of stress in his own breeding programme upon the sterling working qualities that were in the genes of this sporting dog. The Red and White Setter is still worked in the field, and is reckoned by some to be one of the finest bird dogs. It has its own style of pointing, dropping very low to the ground, which is said to be a legacy of the way its ancestors had once worked with nets rather than guns.

Huston made good use of the networking opportunities within his Church, and involved a number of other Presbyterian ministers in his mission to save the Red and

White Setter from extinction. He did not keep systematic and detailed records of his breeding activities, but he did note each of his litters faithfully in the parish register—alongside the human births. According to Anna Redlich, a historian of Irish dogs, 'in due time and by judicious selection' Huston managed to build up a small kennel of purebred dogs. He was not the only breeder of Red and White Setters, but he was the most significant in the first part of the twentieth century. According to one enthusiast, he was 'the undoubted saviour of the lovely animal held so precious today', and some of his better-known dogs can still be found in the pedigrees of present-day champions.

Towards the end of his life, Huston engaged in lengthy correspondence with another dedicated Red and White Setter breeder called Maureen Cuddy. He was able to furnish her with some valuable information about the breeding programme followed by him and his cousin, and through her own detailed research and record-keeping she was able to construct full and accurate pedigrees for the existing purebred dogs. Sadly, Noble Huston did not live long enough to see the foundation of Ireland's first Red and White Setter breed club. He died in 1944, soon after his son had been killed on active service in World War Two, and just a few months before the club was founded. The inscription on his headstone is taken from St Paul's Epistle to the Hebrews: 'He being dead yet speaketh'—which has turned out to be a wholly appropriate epitaph.

In 1940 Maureen Cuddy had been given a sick Red and White Setter pup to look after. She nursed the little bitch back to health, and this proved to be the start of a lifelong connection with the breed. She called the pup

Judith Cunningham of Knockalla (Knockalla was her kennel's name), and although she was only mated once, it seems probable that every living Red and White Setter is descended from this one dog. In the years ahead, Maureen and her husband, William, were to prove instrumental in the campaign to gain recognition for the Red and White Setter breed both inside Ireland and from a range of international kennel clubs.

It was not an easy task: in fact, it required patience, dedication and a good deal of stamina since there were many setbacks. Fortunately, Maureen Cuddy had more than her fair share of all those qualities. According to some reports, however, she received little encouragement from the Irish Kennel Club in her persistent attempts to have the Red and White Setter fully accepted as a separate breed. In one account she 'toiled and foiled' for years with intransigent members of the Kennel Club who seemed to be 'hell-bound to confine her beloved Irish breed to legend and/or oblivion'. No doubt there were some personal factors involved, and Cuddy is said to have encountered 'inconsistencies and animosities' from 'where she should have expected aid'. It has been claimed that some of the breeders of all-red setters were opposed to any form of recognition being accorded to their own dogs' blood relatives—which seems strange, if true, given their subsequent support for cross-breeding programmes.

There are obvious similarities between the two breeds of setter, both in appearance and temperament. They both possess a beautifully proportioned and balanced shape. Both are lean, strong and intelligent specimens. Their coats are both rich and glossy, but never curly. Both breeds are feathered on their front and back legs, and on their tails. The most obvious distinguishing feature between is their colour, which is used to define the breed of each dog. However, there are also some more subtle differences. The Red and White Setter does not quite match the same streamlined frame of its cousin. It tends to be a little smaller and heavier in body, with a broader head. The coat is usually somewhat tighter and shorter than the Red Setter's, which means it can require less trimming and grooming. The temperament of the Red and White Setter is also reckoned to be less volatile, and more easy-going than its close relative.

'It is a phenomenon,' Anna Redlich wrote in her *History of Irish Dogs*, that:

> whenever a nearly extinct breed is resuscitated by painstaking efforts, the public calls the old-timer an unwelcome newcomer, a menace to the standard of dog shows, and to the morals of exhibitors.

She went on to suggest that the followers of the old Red and White Irish Setter may well have experienced some of this antagonism on the 'thorny path that leads to the official recognition of a breed'. Redlich forecast that such opposition would 'gradually give way to reluctant tolerance', and believed that eventually 'antagonists are transformed into advocates and once again all is quiet on the canine front'. Anna Redlich was writing in 1949, and while her predictions proved accurate in some respects, the progress of the Red and White Setters along that 'thorny path' has proved to be more problematic than she had anticipated.

Although the breed managed to survive through the 1950s and 1960s, the future of the Red and White Setter remained precarious—at times, extremely so—and it required periodic and careful outcrossing with all-red dogs. According to Leighton Boyce, this 'weaving in of the mixed material' had been a 'delicate operation requiring rigorous selection', but it helped to ensure that the breed would survive. Maureen Cuddy served as secretary of the breed club throughout those decades, and saw a long-awaited breakthrough take place in the 1970s. She had kept scrupulous records of the breeding that had occurred in previous years, and in 1974, exactly thirty years after she had helped to form the first Red and White Setter Club, she managed to persuade the Irish Kennel Club formally to accept that the pedigrees of the remaining setters were accurate, and that no English Setter blood had been introduced to the breed.

In 1976, the Kennel Club approached the Irish Red Setter Club to help oversee the final stages of the revival of the Red and White Setter, and two years later the breed was formally recognised by the Irish Kennel Club. In 1982 another landmark was passed when a field trial was held for Red and White Setters. It is believed to have been the first such trial for almost a century, and the first ever held under the rules of the Irish Kennel Club. Further outbreeding with all-red setters continued in the following decade. In 1990 the Red and White Setter Society organised the first of nine matings between Red and White and all-red dogs. Each of the setters was chosen because of their type, conformation of standard points, temperament and working ability. The objective was to improve the genetic base of the Red and White Setter 'without compromising any points of the breed'. Each of the pups that were born had to pass exacting standards before they could be registered as pedigree setters with the Kennel Club. It was also expressly stipulated that the dogs must bear no resemblance to the English Setter, 'neither in form nor in mode of work, nor yet particularly with regard to markings'.

In 1977, Maureen Cuddy had bred her last setters, and in so doing performed a final valuable service for the breed. She had mated a Red and White Setter bitch with a Red Setter dog that carried a lot of white colouring. The litter that followed from this union included an outstanding pup called Harlequin of Knockalla. This specimen was bought by an English breeding couple, Alan and Ann Gormley, who exhibited the dog at Crufts in 1980. This type of setter was almost unknown in Britain at the time—indeed, many people thought the breed had already become extinct. The showing sparked off renewed interest in Red and White Setters, and the Gormleys obtained another pup from Maureen Cuddy, a bitch this time, who was bred twice with Harlequin. Their pups proved influential in the development of the Red and White Setter in the UK, and led to the formation of a breed club in Britain in 1983. Not long afterwards the breed was recognised by the British Kennel Club and by the Fédération Cynologique Internationale.

The Irish Setter had not only caught the attention of those in the UK. In the 1980s, breeding pairs of Red and White Setters were imported to the United States. During the decades that followed there was a gradual increase in their numbers. Eventually, in 2009, the Red and White Setter was fully recognised by the American Kennel Club, and deemed eligible to compete in all fields. By then the Irish dog had been recognised by most of the world's national kennels, and had competed in a range of conformation shows and field trials, winning awards in both disciplines. The future of the breed seemed more viable than it had in over a century. However, the number of Red and White Setters remained low, with fewer than one hundred registered each year in the UK, and there were other critical issues that would soon arise for the owners and breeders of all pedigree dogs.

In order to validate pedigrees and identities, the British Kennel Club had established a Stud Book in 1887, in which owners could record the pedigree of their individual dog or kennel. This book soon became of vital importance to the selling and buying of dogs, since proof of breeding could greatly increase an animal's value. As a consequence, the Kennel Club came to exert a good deal of both creative and commercial influence. It seems indisputable that there was also a kind of gravitational pull towards the idea of physical perfection in each breed. On one hand, there was considerable support for greater clarity in the definition of the various breeds. On the other hand, the standards set by judging panels could sometimes seem arbitrary, with uncertain long-term implications for the health of pedigree dogs. Even in the 1880s, concerns were expressed about the physical and psychological impact on smaller breeds caused by the constant demands to reduce their size.

So long as stud books are kept open, it allows the gene pool of any breed to be increased through the practice of outcrossing with other types of dog. When stud books are said to be closed, it means that dogs whose pedigrees show evidence of recent cross-breeding will not be accepted to compete in any dog shows that are organised by a national kennel club. In cases where there is a relatively small gene pool for a particular breed to draw upon, this stricture clearly increases the possibility of genetic disorders being passed on to future generations. Some of these, such as hip dyslexia or Von Willebrand Disease (vWD), are found more often in large-breed dogs. Other conditions, such as progressive retinal atrophy and epilepsy, are thought to be distributed among a much wider range of pedigree breeds.

It should be acknowledged that some breeders believe that there is little difference in the overall health of pedigree and mongrel animals, and that the reason purebred dogs are more associated with genetic illness is simply because their owners are more likely to take them to vets for regular check-ups. That view is not accepted by everyone, and the issues that selective breeding raises for the health of some pedigree dogs were explored in 2008 in a controversial BBC documentary that was to affect the future of dog breeding, not only in the United Kingdom, but also in Ireland and further afield.

Scandal

The BBC documentary was called *Pedigree Dogs Exposed*, and it proved to be a highly influential (indeed, a landmark) event in the recent history of pedigree dog-breeding. The programme held the British Kennel Club to account for permitting, and even encouraging, breeding practices that had compromised the health of some purebred specimens. The documentary included harrowing footage of the effects that extreme inbreeding could produce, and this provoked a sense of horror and outrage among the general public. It led various sponsors, including the Royal Society for the Prevention of Cruelty to Animals and the Dogs Trust, to withdraw their support for the Crufts annual show, as well as other events run by the British Kennel Club. The programme also caused the BBC to abandon its long tradition of providing extensive TV coverage of Crufts. This coverage is the cornerstone of the whole dog-breeding industry in the UK, and the BBC's decision had obvious financial implications, and not just for British dog-breeders.

The BBC documentary was not without its faults. It suggested, for example, that the ridge on Rhodesian Ridgebacks was a symptom of inherited spina bifida, which it is not. On the other hand, it revealed that the official policy of the Rhodesian Ridgeback Club was to cull any puppy born without a ridge, which shocked many viewers. It could be argued that the documentary did not present an entirely objective view of its subject, and failed to acknowledge the commitment and progress that had been made within the breeding industry to eliminate some genetic defects, which is, after all, clearly in the breeders' long-term interests. Nonetheless, it offered a powerful critique of the dangers of an obsessive focus on breed purity; of the toleration of dangerous degrees of close inbreeding; and of the overuse of show-winning sires. Although the findings of the documentary were hotly disputed at the time of its transmission by the Kennel Club (which dismissed it as 'unfair' and 'highly biased'), they led directly to three major enquiries into the scale of the problem, and then to suggested reforms. These led, in turn, to significant changes in the practice of pedigree dog-breeding.

The changes included a comprehensive review by the British Kennel Club of all breed standards, with a new emphasis placed upon the need to reward breeders who showed healthy dogs. Bans on close inbreeding were also introduced, and new standards were set for very many breeds. It was promised that those standards would not 'include anything that could in any way be interpreted as encouraging features that might prevent a dog from breathing, walking and seeing freely'. The impact of these and other reforms have been felt throughout the global canine industry.

None of Ireland's native breeds was identified in the BBC documentary as among the worst cases of genetic defects produced by limited gene pools. However, that does not mean they have been unaffected by the pressures of breeding outstanding specimens for the exhibition ring. According to David Hancock, the Irish Red Setter show-dog now tends to be lacking in basic muscular development, particularly, in its hindquarters. This, he believes, is 'not a pretty sight' in dogs that were 'once revered the world over for their stamina'. In fact, this sort of criticism goes back a very long way. As early as 1890, one critic wrote that 'breeders of the Irish Red Setter for show purposes have sacrificed the grand old powerful big-boned animal for the sake of beauty'. Somewhat similar criticisms have been made about some of the other Irish breeds, such as the Kerry Blue and the Irish Wolfhound.

Following the screening of the BBC documentary, the gene pools that supplied pedigree dogs like the Red and White Setters with their bloodlines were subjected to a greatly increased level of scrutiny. The Irish Kennel Club was, of course, aware that all of the world's Red and White Setters were descended from a small number of dogs, and decided to see if there was any significant difference between their current bloodlines. This investigation confirmed the limited size of the gene pool, and revealed that their bloodlines often connected siblings; grandparents had been mated with grandchildren; and some individual dogs turned up in multiple lines.

Although Red and White Setters are generally very healthy, some known problems have featured in the recent history of the dog, possibly as a result of inbreeding. One of those is the CLAD mutation, which compromises the canine immune system. Another is the vWD mutation, which causes blood to fail to clot. In both these cases, kennel clubs will only register those setters that are proven by DNA testing to be free of either mutation. Thanks to the rigour of this approach, CLAD and vWD are very rarely present in this breed of dog.

Nonetheless, the Irish Kennel Club felt there was too much inbreeding of Red and White Setters, and wished to extend the gene pool by outcrossing with Red Setters, whose genes, after all, are very similar. That programme was supported by the Irish Red and White Setter Club of Ireland, and by the Irish Red Setter Club (Ireland). However, outcrossing was not welcomed by all of the Red and White Setter breed clubs in the world. The Canadian club stated that it could not 'condone the cross-breeding of our essentially healthy breed with dogs of a breed which is known to hold, by various unknown modes of inheritance, far more genetic detritus than ours'. The British Club also felt that the outcross was neither desirable nor necessary.

What may have concerned some club members is the anxiety that cross-breeding with all-red setters could, over time, reduce the points of distinction between the two types of Irish dog, and diminish the status of the Red and White Setter as a separate breed. It had taken so many years for this setter to win official recognition that I can understand and sympathise with that reaction. Some breeders have also expressed concern that solid red dogs could pop up in red and white litters in several generations' time, and that might have damaging financial implications for their kennels. Others have come close to suggesting that interbreeding will result in a mongrel dog that is neither one type nor the other. I think that is most unlikely—provided that the crosses are organised properly and well monitored.

I also feel that such objections overlook the fact that there are already red dogs in the ancestry and DNA of every Red and White Setter—and, of course, the reverse is equally true. In fact, the bloodlines of other breeds of setter may also be present. Writing in the 1920s, Colonel J. K. Milner referred to the presence of what he termed 'alien' setters that had arrived in Ireland 'with the railways and the steamers'. He appears to be referring to Gordon Setters, since he claimed that the influence of this 'new blood' led to the colour of the Irish breeds becoming darker. There may be little written documentation of breeding between the different types and colours of Irish Setter that took place in past centuries. However, that may only have been because the different types were not considered to constitute separate breeds, and so their mating with each other was not thought worth recording. In fact, as the Irish Kennel Club has pointed out, it was the shared ancestry between the two Irish Setters that enabled the revival of the Red and White Setter in the first place.

In any case, Irish sportsmen in the eighteenth and early nineteenth centuries would have been more likely to assess dogs by their performance in the field than by the colour of their coats. The Rossmore family may have been known for their reluctance to breed their Red and White Setters with all-reds, but the fact that this reluctance was noted by their contemporaries clearly implies that it was exceptional. It was only from the mid nineteenth century, as we shall see, that the division between the all-red and Red and White Irish Setters was deemed to be definitive.

David Hancock has suggested that it would be good for setters if the colours that define their breeds were simply to be ignored, and interbreeding between all setter dogs, not just the Irish, were to be permitted. That would certainly enlarge the gene pool, but it seems unlikely to happen—there are simply too many people dedicated to preserving and promoting each setter breed. However, we have at least moved forwards from the time when the culling of pups on the basis of their colour was practised extensively. If the result of this latest outcrossing programme means that future generations of Red and White Setter dogs are less likely to suffer from pain and disease, then I think that the price is well worth paying.

The outbreeding programme for Red and White Setters that was instituted by the Irish Kennel Club was thorough and well planned. However, some have argued that the slate of reforms promised by the British Kennel Club represent a mere cosmetic exercise. They have claimed that professional dog-breeders are inextricably locked into a system that cannot be reformed, since it is one that offers the greatest rewards to breeders whose dogs meet the most exacting standards of physical appearance, regardless of the impact that might have on the health and well-being of the animals. They contend that this can only lead to more inbreeding, which will in turn increase the likelihood of further genetic disorders emerging. According to the prominent Hungarian ethologist Vilmos Csányi, that process now appears to be 'unstoppable' for most pedigree breeds.

Crufts, as the world's premier shop window for dog breeds, continues to come under fire for its role in the development of certain pedigree dogs. In 2016, criticism focused on the German Shepherd specimen that had won its breed class at the Crufts show. The dog in question was described as having a 'sloping back' and a 'deformed gait'. Once again, the issue of questionable breeding practices was raised, and on this occasion Michele Hanson, a *Guardian* journalist, seemed to attach some of the blame directly to the Irish. 'In Ireland,' she wrote, 'you can apparently do more or less what you like with dogs.' She claimed that this explained why there were so many 'horrible puppy farms' in Ireland, which were 'licensed by councils', and were 'churning out sick dogs'.

Michele Hanson has written movingly about the rescue dog that she adopted, and for whom she clearly feels deep affection. However, some of her accusations in this *Guardian* article seemed poorly researched, ill-informed and quite unfair. She appeared to believe, for example, that the

The initial appeal of the Irish Wolfhound, as bred by Captain Graham, was primarily to Ireland's landed gentry, who had enough room and financial resources to maintain the giant dog. That may explain why some radical Nationalists wished to replace the Wolfhound as Ireland's National Dog with the Kerry Blue Terrier, a breed that they deemed to be 'racy and of the soil'.

This Wolfhound pup is only a few months old, but is already as large as some fully grown dogs. Despite its great size and relatively short life expectancy, the Wolfhound is one of only three native Irish breeds that are not currently considered to be vulnerable to extinction.

Captain George Graham may have seemed like a typical English country gentleman of the Victorian age. However, he devoted half a century of his life to the goal of resurrecting the ancient Irish Wolfhound. He is pictured here towards the start of his mission, standing beside a model of his ideal specimen. Graham's relentless dedication, personal wealth and influential social connections helped to create and popularise the modern breed.

Two young Irish Wolfhounds at an all-breed show in Dublin in 2016. Often viewed as the most iconic of all Irish dogs, the modern Wolfhound was created in rural Gloucestershire in the late nineteenth century by Captain George Graham, and includes Danish, Scottish, Russian and Tibetan breeds among its many ancestors.

The goal of resurrecting the Irish Wolfhound, many years after the breed was believed to have become extinct, coincided with other ambitions of the cultural movement in Ireland that became known as the Celtic Revival. This romantic movement sought to restore the supposed traditions—the sports, the language, the decorative arts and even the fashions—of Celtic Ireland before the country was conquered and colonised by the English.

This Kerry Blue Terrier came third at a show in Killarney in 1916. At that time, the breed was considered 'racy, and of the soil', which may explain its appeal to radical Irish Nationalists. This specimen may seem to have few similarities with the modern show dog. However, within a few years of this photo being taken, the Kerry Blue had become popular in the UK and USA, and the breed had begun to develop the highly groomed and stylised appearance by which it is known today.

This photo of Kerry Blue Terriers was taken in 1921. At that time, the breed was approaching the height of its popularity in Ireland. It was the favourite dog of the Republican leader, Michael Collins, and had acquired a following among those young men who shared his political views. Collins planned to introduce legislation that would have made the Kerry Blue the National Dog of Ireland, but he was assassinated in 1922 before his plans could be realised.

Kerry Blues were reputed to be the only dogs capable of killing an otter 'single-handed, and in deep water'. Their use in otter hunts continued well into the twentieth century. This photo from the 1920s shows the outcome of one such hunt. Since otters are now an endangered species, they are no longer hunted in Ireland.

The colour of this Kerry Blue Terrier is still closer to black than blue, but that is likely to change as she grows older. This young bitch already displays the highly stylised cut that was developed in the 1920s, and is now always given to the Kerry Blue show dog.

This Irish Red Setter pup in County Wexford is just eight weeks old, but already she displays the beautifully proportioned features of the mature dog, including the expression that was described by Harry Blake Knox in 1866 as 'kind, sensible and loving'.

The Red and White Setter was believed by some Irish breeders to be a better gun dog than its all-red cousin. That was, in part, because the dog was thought to be less volatile than the red breed, with better hunting instincts. Its white colouring also made it easier to follow against the dark heather and bog of the Irish countryside.

Irish dogs have often been used to brand products. In the last century, an Irish Red Setter was used to advertise this tobacco plant in Limerick. Garryowen was a famous champion dog, owned by a relation of James Joyce. Some believe that he served as a model for the 'mangy mongrel' featured in Joyce's *Ulysses*.

In 1876, an Irish Red Setter called Elcho became the first Irish Red Setter to win a championship event in the USA. He had been imported from Ireland, and his grand-sire was William Hutchinson's dog Bob. Elcho went on to sire 197 pups of his own, and is believed to be the ancestor of almost every Irish Red Setter now living in the USA. This is one of his sons, Elcho Jr., who also became a show champion.

An eight-week-old Irish Red Setter pup from County Wexford.

In order to maintain the Red and White Setter breed, there have been a number of breeding programmes in which they have been crossed with Red Setters. The most recent cross-breeding programme instigated by the Irish Kennel Club has produced some beautiful specimens like this one, and seems to have ensured the future genetic diversity of the breed.

Attempts to maintain the Red and White Setter breed are not confined to Ireland. This pup was bred in Minnesota in the USA, where the Red and White Setter is widely regarded as one of the best breeds of bird dogs.

It was not until the nineteenth century that the appearance of sporting dogs began to be given as much consideration as their abilities in the field, and colour became an issue of vital importance to breeders. From that point, the all-red setter began to grow rapidly in popularity, and the numbers of Red and White Setters began to decline.

THE IRISH RED AND WHITE SETTER OF 1840
from the *Naturalist's Library*

In the 1840s, the Red and White Setter was still the most common setter found in Ireland. By the 1880s, however, its popularity had been eclipsed by its close relative: the all-red dog. In the following century the breed was on the verge of extinction on several occasions, but thanks to the remarkable dedication of breeders such as the Presbyterian minister Noble Huston, Irish Red and White Setters have managed to survive.

This photo was taken in 1934, and marks the first dog show in which Glen of Imaal Terriers were allowed to compete. Until 1966, these terriers were also tested on their abilities to draw live badgers from their setts. The Glens had to hold and work the badgers for six minutes without losing their grip, and if they made any sound during that struggle they were deemed to have failed the test.

The Glen of Imaal Terrier is Ireland's only dwarf breed, and was bred to hunt in silence. The terrier was developed in the isolated Glen of Imaal, probably by the descendants of soldiers from Cromwell's Model Army who had been given land in County Wicklow. Now, it is the rarest of Ireland's native terriers.

The Glen of Imaal has sometimes been described as a 'big dog on short legs'. This terrier has three growth stages, and can take up to four years to reach full maturity, by which time the dog is very muscular, with powerful hindquarters. The Glen's limbs may be short, but their chests, hips and bones are actually larger than those of many non-dwarf breeds.

Three generations of Irish Water Spaniel are portrayed in this print from the 1880s. The Water Spaniel may be the oldest of Ireland's native dogs. Unlike some of them, this breed has changed very little in appearance since the 1830s, when it was first fixed in the Dublin kennels of Justin McCarthy. Nowadays, there are reckoned to be fewer than 400 Water Spaniels in the whole of Ireland, and Irish breeders often have to look abroad if they wish to preserve genetic diversity.

The face of Boatswain, an Irish Water Spaniel born in Dublin in 1832. It is believed that Justin McCarthy bred Boatswain out of both the northern and southern strains of this water dog. Boatswain lived for eighteen years, and sired numerous pups in that time. In this and other respects, he may properly be regarded as the father of the modern breed.

The 'amber eyes' of Maria, an Irish Water Spaniel, captivated Captain Yeates, the hero of Somerville and Ross's 'Irish R.M.' stories. At the time their stories were written, the spaniel was one of the most popular of Irish breeds around the world. Since then its popularity has been eclipsed, both as a hunting dog and as a family pet, by the Labrador Retriever.

This Irish Water Spaniel pup has still to acquire her mature colouring and distinctive coat. The spaniel is now one of the rarest of all the Irish breeds, even in its native country. Most of the pups in this litter were bound for homes outside Ireland.

This early print of an Irish Terrier shows a dog whose ears have been cropped. A judge at a show in Belfast in 1882 predicted 'a popular future' for the breed if they could be 'produced with ears that do not require cutting'. Ear-cropping was soon forbidden by the terrier's breed club, and before long the practice became unacceptable in many other breeds. Nowadays, the dog's ears are trained to be folded forwards.

An Irish Terrier on a show bench in County Down in 2016. This lovely young bitch displays the 'three R's' thought by William Graham of Newtownbreda, County Antrim, to be essential to the breed: she is 'Red, Racy and Rectangular'.

During World War One, many Irish Terriers served in the Allied trenches carrying messages, scouting enemy positions and catching vermin. Paddy (above) was attached to a New Zealand battalion, and saw action on the beaches of Gallipoli and in the trenches of the Western Front. Unlike many in his regiment, Paddy managed to survive the war and was able to return home. However, this breed's association with the British Army was not to the liking of some Irish Nationalists.

A young Kerry Beagle pup. Not all members of the breed share this distinctive black and tan colouring, and not all Kerry Beagles take part in fox-hunting. In recent years there has been a growth in the popularity of drag hunts, which may offer a more secure future to a breed that has been threatened with extinction for over 100 years.

The Kerry Beagle was once the principal breed used for fox-hunting by the Irish gentry, with some families keeping packs of up to 200 dogs. In the course of the nineteenth century, however, these scent hounds became victims of the bitter conflict between tenants and their landlords. When this picture was painted in the 1930s, almost all of the old family packs had been dispersed. Today, only one remains: the Scarteen pack in County Limerick.

The Kerry Beagle is Ireland's only scent hound. The breed has a highly developed sense of smell, and is still primarily used for the purpose for which it was originally bred: hunting. In the past, the Kerry Beagle has seldom competed in breed shows, which may explain why it is not a recognised breed outside Ireland. In recent years, however, the dog has begun to appear more often in championship events.

The Soft-Coated Wheaten Terrier is probably the oldest of all of Ireland's native terrier breeds. Curiously, it was also the last Irish terrier to be recognised as a distinct and separate breed. Since then, it has become the most popular of the native terriers—both inside and outside Ireland—and is currently the only one that is not considered to be facing possible extinction.

These two Irish Soft-Coated Wheaten dogs with docked tails come from the 1940s, not long after this terrier had been recognised as a distinct breed by the Irish Kennel Club. Despite claims that the Wheaten has hardly changed over the centuries, these dogs seem noticeably different—in styling, at least—from today's show breed. However, their coat and colour seem consistent.

These three pups show the dark markings that are frequently seen around the muzzles of the Wheaten Terrier when they are newly born. In time, most of this will fade, and the dogs will gain the colouring by which the breed is known.

Many terriers have double coats to protect them from harsh weather, but the Irish Wheaten has a single wavy coat that can appear to flow as the dog moves, and is soft to the touch. The American strain of Wheaten has developed a woollier coat, but the Irish dog is still the breed standard. This lovely bitch is almost seventeen years old, but still enjoys her daily walks in Dublin's Churchtown.

docking of dogs' tails was still perfectly legal in Ireland. In fact, the Veterinary Council of Ireland deems it unethical for vets to carry out tail-docking for cosmetic or prophylactic purposes, and considers this to be an 'act of mutilation'. It is also illegal for anyone else to perform this procedure. The issue of puppy farming in Ireland is real and serious, but the chief offenders are those who operate outside the law, not those who have obtained licences, and whose businesses are, therefore, open to inspection and regulation.

Having said that, there is no room for undue satisfaction on this front. Tens of thousands of pups are still produced every year in Irish puppy farms, mainly for export, and in some kennels breeding bitches have been housed like battery hens, and kept in a state of almost constant pregnancy. There is also little excuse for the prolonged delays and lack of urgency that successive Irish governments have shown in addressing this issue. New legislation now includes better provisions for animal welfare, breeding limits, kennel sizes, exercise areas, and socialisation of animals. There is also now a requirement for some degree of staff training, and more exacting standards of record keeping have been introduced. However, this legislation does not include a limit on the number of dogs a puppy farmer can keep for breeding purposes. Some Irish 'farms' now house more than 500 dogs, and it is very hard to believe that each of them can receive the care and attention they deserve.

It should also be acknowledged that advances in genetic science now allow breeders the possibility of running DNA tests that can identify those dogs that are most likely to pass on affected genes. In time, this may enable the excessive inbreeding that can cause deformity or illness to be countered and reversed. Of course, that depends on the commitment of both individual breeders and their national kennel clubs if it is to prove effective.

It is worth pointing out again that there is not a complete consensus among veterinary scientists that pedigree dogs are invariably less healthy than cross-breeds or mongrels. Some recent research found that purebred dogs are no more likely than cross-breeds to suffer from the most common medical conditions, such as heart murmurs, problems with their joints and teeth and gum diseases. These findings contradict the widely held view that purebred dogs are inherently unhealthy because of selective breeding. The research was funded by the RSPCA, and it found that, while there could be a prevalence of some disorders in certain pedigree breeds, there was no significant difference in their general health when they were compared to a group of cross-breeds.

There are, of course, some animal activists who consider any form of selective breeding to be reminiscent of the murderous eugenics programmes instituted in the 1930s and 1940s by Nazi Germany. According to A. J. Alba, judging any animals by their appearance draws upon the same abhorrent reasoning that led to 'separate drinking fountains and bans on interracial marriages, and is akin to saying that whites are better than blacks'.

It may be true that contemporary dog-breeders sometimes employ the language that was once used by racial eugenicists in the nineteenth and early twentieth centuries, such as the claim that certain bloodlines can and should be considered as 'purer' than others. Francis Galton, who originated the term 'eugenics', even proposed that dog-breeding techniques provided a model that could be adapted and applied to humans in order to produce an ideal ruling elite (and, presumably, an equivalent and acquiescent underclass). It is also true that the growth of modern dog shows in Europe roughly coincided with that of modern racist ideology. However, the systematic breeding of dogs clearly predates contemporary racism by several millennia, and direct comparisons between the two activities obscure much more than they reveal.

Indeed, according to a paper written by a team of biologists which appeared in a 2004 edition of *Science*, the breeding of the domestic dog is 'a genetic enterprise' on a vast scale that is 'unique in human history'. There is no agreement as to when humans began this complex process, but it is believed to be somewhere between 10,000 and 30,000 years ago—and possibly even longer. In that sense, every type of dog, whether pedigree, cross-breed or mongrel, is equally 'ancient'. The powerful impulse that compels humans to design dogs—for a mix of practical, emotional and aesthetic reasons—also seems to have been a constant factor over the same extended period. There can be little doubt that the domestication of dogs marked a profound turning point in human history, which has even been compared in importance to the discovery of fire. It would be surprising if the breeding of dogs that has taken place over thousands of years had not produced some negative effects, as well as many positive ones.

In the case of the Red and White Setter, I think that the actions of the Irish Kennel Club have been both prudent and preemptive. Thankfully, none of Ireland's native breeds displays the worst symptoms of excessive inbreeding. Nonetheless, one of them has been bred deliberately to perpetuate a fundamental genetic defect.

Little Big Dog: the Glen of Imaal Terrier

There are a number of small dogs in the world, but relatively few that may be considered as genuine dwarf breeds. Individual dogs can suffer from dwarfism, but there are certain breeds that were created by design to be short-legged. This was usually not done for cosmetic reasons, or because anyone thought it would make them look more appealing or cute: they were bred that way in order to be better equipped to meet the demands of the job that they were required to do. Just one of Ireland's dogs falls into this category, and it is Ireland's rarest terrier. The form of dwarfism that occurs in the Glen of Imaal Terrier is called micromelic achondroplasia, which means that the Glens have short legs, but in all other respects are standard sized.

Dwarf breeds of dog have an ancient history, and they have normally been bred that way in order to enable them to go underground to catch small and medium-sized mammals. Their short legs help them to enter a sett and confront what can be a tough and aggressive quarry, such as a badger. The Glen's legs also allow it to be followed by its owner on foot, and to stay close and avoid flying hooves when they are herding other animals. Short dogs, as opposed to small ones, have been developed in many countries, and it is believed that most of them share the same genetic mutation. This causes their leg bones to be shortened, and their front legs to be somewhat bowed and turned outwards.

The achondroplastic breed that developed in Ireland originated in, and is named after, the Glen of Imaal in County Wicklow. There are three glens in Wicklow, and Imaal is the most isolated and remote of the three. It is ringed by steep mountains, and is now used as a firing range by the Irish Army, which has ensured that there are very few, if any, Glen of Imaal Terriers to be found in the Glen of Imaal.

There are varied explanations of how the terrier breed got there in the first place. The dog's history may have begun during the reign of Queen Elizabeth I, who hired French and Hessian mercenaries to suppress the rebellion of Gaelic chieftain Hugh O'Neill. After the Nine Years' War was over, some of those soldiers are thought to have settled in the Wicklow area. They may have brought hounds with them of the dwarf basset type, which they bred with the local terrier stock, eventually creating a new and distinctive breed. The low-slung hounds that are believed to figure in the Glen's ancestry may also be connected to other dwarf breeds.

I think the Glens' ancestors are most likely to have been brought to Wicklow by the soldiers of Cromwell's New Model Army. Many of his 'Ironsides' (cavalry soldiers) were owed substantial arrears in pay by the time they had ended their military campaign in Ireland, and Cromwell paid them in Irish land. He wanted to extend the Pale area around Dublin (the stronghold of English influence in Ireland) into the neighbouring county of Wicklow, and so it was there that many of his soldiers were granted acres of land. Most of those soldiers had no experience of farming, and some of the land they had been given was very poor: rocky, uneven and infertile. Within a few years, the bulk of Cromwell's settlers had returned to England. Those that were left tried to scratch a living from the stony soil, and would have welcomed a dog like the Glen that could catch small game and bring more food to their tables. According to other accounts, the dwarf breed was introduced to Wicklow by Huguenot immigrants—French Protestants who came to Ireland to escape oppression in their own country, and brought their dogs with them.

It is, of course, also possible that the Glen Terrier simply developed from a genetic mutation in the local dogs that eventually 'bred true' because of the Glen of Imaal's isolated location. This was, after all, a period when travel was often difficult inside Ireland, and Dubliners would sometimes refer to 'journeying to the interior' when they moved outside the Pale. Until the end of the nineteenth century, the terrier remained secluded, and not only from the rest of the world: the breed was hardly known even within Ireland. However, it seems that the Glen is probably related to other Irish terriers such as the Soft-Coated Wheaten and the Kerry Blue. More surprising is that DNA analysis shows that the Glen is closely connected with the Molosser, a canine group that is mainly composed of some very large breeds, such as Mastiffs, and which originates in a region of southern Europe that now straddles Greece and Albania.

It is not clear how that connection might have been made, but it may help to explain why the Glen is sometimes characterised as a 'big dog on short legs'. Certainly, the Irish dog is a more substantial specimen than might be expected from its height. It has three growth stages, and it can take up to four years for this terrier to reach full maturity, but by then it can weigh more than forty pounds. It is also very muscular and extremely strong, with powerful hindquarters. In fact, the strength in its hindquarters is so pronounced that it makes the top line of the dog appear to rise towards its rear. Glens have large heads in proportion to their bodies. This is because dwarf dogs have braincases that are normally just as big as those in larger breeds. In other words, the reduction in their body size is not reflected in their brains—or in their intelligence, for that matter. Essentially, the Glens are not small dogs: their limbs may be short, but their chests, hips and bones are actually larger than many non-dwarf breeds.

The Glen's low centre of gravity allows the dog to perform what is known as the 'Glen sit'. Unlike most breeds, this terrier can rest comfortably on its rear end, and hold its whole body vertical for long periods of time. In the past, the dog's tail was docked to a length just sufficient to serve as a handhold for pulling the dog out of a badger sett. Docking is still standard in the United States, but Ireland has banned the exhibition of any breed whose tails were docked on or after 6 March 2014.

Like most terriers, Glens were originally used for eradicating vermin, for hunting badgers and foxes, and as a general-purpose farm dog. However, unlike most other terriers, they were bred to work in silence. They went 'mute to ground', and would enter dens and setts without making any noise. The Glens were often used in conjunction with other terriers. A small dog would be sent into a badger's sett, and would bark to tell its owner that the prey had been found.

The hunter would then dig down to the first dog, and remove it from the sett. Next, the Glen would be sent down to drag the badger out. Badgers can sometimes weigh more than sixty pounds, and are often ferocious when cornered, so the Glen needed to be of a substantial weight, with strong shoulders and a very powerful bite. Great determination and courage were also needed since badgers would wage a life-or-death struggle to avoid coming to the surface. During this battle, the Glen would remain silent. Indeed, in hunting trials, which used to be demanded by many clubs, Glens were disqualified if they sounded at the quarry. In cases when the Glens were mauled or even killed by badgers, they still managed to remain silent.

Glen of Imaal Terriers were once required to earn a '*Teastas Misneach*' ('Certificate of Courage') before they were allowed to enter a championship show in Ireland. This involved the Glen being able to draw a badger from its sett, silently and within a specified time. The dog was released into a maze of winding tunnels, and had just one minute to find the badger. The dog then had to pull the badger out of the tunnel, and, naturally, the badger would fight fiercely to prevent that from happening. The Glen had to hold and work the badger for six minutes without losing its grip, and without making a sound if the certificate were to be awarded. It may seem hard to credit that not only did this grotesque form of badger-baiting persist in Ireland until well into the twentieth century, but it was allowed and approved by the Irish Kennel Club. Thankfully, these barbaric trials have been forbidden since 1966.

As a result of their breeding, Glen terriers still tend to be quiet dogs and seldom bark, but when they do it is the full-throated sound of a large dog, surprising those who expected the sound to be in proportion to their overall size. Some of the

Glen's features were common in the early generations of other breeds of terrier, but have not proved popular in the show ring, and have been bred out of them. Since the Glen did not feature in shows until a relatively late stage, it avoided such genteel improvements. For that reason, the Glen is sometimes referred to as an 'unrefined' breed.

Some people believe that the Glen may also have been used as a 'turnspit dog'. The traditional method of roasting meat was on a spit stretched across an open fire. This required someone to turn the meat over a period of several hours to ensure that it was cooked evenly. Instead of employing a servant for this tedious labour, kitchens in larger homes would install a small treadmill, which was sometimes part of a barrel or a wheel. This would serve as a kind of running track for a dog, and as the animal ran, the spit would turn. The same device could also be adapted to churn butter. Although larger dogs were sometimes used in this mechanism, for obvious reasons it worked best with a short-legged breed, and the Glen's low front and strong hindquarters made it well suited to this chore.

It is believed that very few turnspit dogs managed to survive into the twentieth century once technology had rendered their occupation obsolete—indeed, they were thought by many to be extinct—and some deny that Glens ever worked in that capacity. Even the suggestion that Glens could once have been employed on the turnspit infuriates some of the breed's current owners. 'Only someone who has never owned a Glen could say that,' one indignant breeder told me. 'This breed is far too smart and far too spirited to have ever been used in that way.' Nonetheless, at the very least, it seems credible, and that may also help to explain the lack of interest taken by show breeders in developing the Glen along more 'refined' lines. Perhaps the previous occupation of the Glens was considered too humble. Perhaps their diminutive stature was not considered impressive enough. At any rate, they seldom featured in early dog shows, and it could be argued that this resulted in the breed remaining true to its original 'antique' type.

Glen terriers have a unique double coat on their back, which is wiry, but with a soft undercoat. However, the head, flanks and legs of the dogs have only the softer coat. The colour may be wheaten, blue or brindled, and Glen pups often have what has been called a 'dorsal stripe' running down their backs, which usually disappears at the onset of adulthood. The Glen terrier does not shed much, and its coat only needs to be brushed or combed every week or two to keep in good condition. Although some extra grooming usually occurs before the dog is exhibited, Glens are allowed to have a somewhat rough and ready appearance when they enter the show ring, so grooming usually requires less effort than with many other breeds. Glens are supposed to look natural, and their coats are never highly stylised in the manner of Irish Terriers. That may be because the frame underneath their coats is not so elegant or well defined.

Glen Terriers are usually kept as domestic pets nowadays, but they have retained some of their old instincts. Most of them have developed an impulse to hunt by the time they reach maturity, and, given the opportunity, they will chase and kill any vermin that crosses their path. They have also been known to chase otters, but they are not strong swimmers since their legs are so short, and their body weight is dense. The breed almost died out at the end of the nineteenth century, and it was only through the devotion of a small number of owners that it managed to survive. It is, perhaps, revealing that there is no charismatic individual like the Reverend Noble Huston, or General Michael Collins, to whom the survival or popularity of the breed can be ascribed. Even though the terrier has been recognised and shown for many years now, that may also help to explain why it is still not well known—even in Ireland. Indeed, in some respects, the Glen may still be considered the 'poor relation' of Ireland's other native breeds. It does not seem surprising that when Ireland's Department of Posts and Telegraphs issued a series of stamps in 1983 that was devoted to Irish dogs, an image of the diminutive Glen did not feature on any of them.

Glen Terriers do not have the glamour of Red Setters, or the physical presence of Wolfhounds. Instead, they have been known as 'the working man's dog', tough and sturdy, and as unpretentious as many of their owners. They may not be big, but they still seem to be the antithesis of every primped and pampered lapdog. That may be part of the reason that it took some time for their breed to be recognised by the Irish Kennel Club. This did not occur until 1934, and Glens first appeared in a show ring the following year. The current standard was approved by the Irish Kennel Club in 1997, and they are now recognised by a number of other national clubs—including the American Kennel Club, which finally granted them recognition in 2004. Glen Terriers are also seen regularly at American Rare Breeds Association shows.

It has to be acknowledged that there are some critics who hold that it is unconscionable to continue to breed a terrier that was designed to be achondroplastic. They claim that there are no scenarios in which dwarf dogs can exist without some cost to the animals, and they have accused breeders of placing the maintenance of the breeds above the health and welfare of their dogs.

It is true that dwarf breeds are associated with higher rates of certain medical conditions, such as arthritis, growth plate injuries, disc disease and ligament damage, than those found in most standard breeds. These are real concerns that need to be taken seriously, and critics of the dwarf breeds recommend two principal responses. These are either to stop, with immediate effect, any further breeding from the existing dwarf dogs, or to cross-breed them with non-dwarf stock so that the length of their legs can be increased and their body shapes altered over a period of time. Both of those options would lead to the extinction of the Glen of Imaal Terrier breed as it is currently recognised.

The Glen Terrier, however, does not display the same extreme effects of achondroplasia as some other dwarf breeds. In the case of Dachshunds, for example, there is a considerably enhanced risk of back problems due to their extremely long spinal columns and their very short ribcages, and that is why around one in four Dachshunds will develop intervertebral diseases. That is only one of a number of medical problems that that dog is likely to face: the others include epilepsy, several types of eye condition and heart disease. The Basset Hound is also highly susceptible to hip and spinal injuries, causing some of these dogs to be euthanised at an early age. They are also open to opportunistic infections in their ears, eyes, and in the folds of skin around their mouths.

Happily, the Glen Terrier is not exposed to the same health risks as those dwarf breeds. On average, the

Irish dogs live from twelve to fourteen years—a healthy lifespan—and suffer from relatively few inherited health problems. However, because they are achondroplastic, Glens can be susceptible to growth difficulties that affect the early development of their front leg bones, and owners are normally advised to discourage their Glens from jumping off sofas or beds in the first year of their lives. While achondroplasia can also be associated with back and weight problems, the overall health of the Glen of Imaal Terrier breed is regarded as good, and they can expect an excellent quality of life. The defective gene that causes this form of dwarfism is not related to their temperament or character in any way.

There is, however, another issue that may compromise the long-term future of this breed, and that involves the numbers of Glen Terriers, or the lack of them, that are currently in the world. There are now reckoned to be no more than thirty breeding bitches in the UK, with fewer than fifty pups registered with the Kennel Club in any year. Given that the threshold for any breed to be considered 'vulnerable' by the Kennel Club is fewer than 300 pups a year, it seems likely that there will be a problem in the future for these terriers to maintain sustainable numbers. There are only around 500 Glen Terriers in the whole of the United States, and the terrier is also listed by the American Kennel Club as one of its ten most endangered breeds. In total, there are reckoned to be only about 2,500 Glens spread throughout the world, and by any standard that represents a very small gene pool.

The English Bulldog is not a dwarf breed, but it does illustrate the dangers of breeding when there is not enough genetic diversity. Inbreeding has already caused some very significant health problems for the Bulldog. Today, artificial insemination is a frequent necessity, since male Bulldogs encounter practical difficulties in mounting a bitch. Should insemination succeed, more than 80 per cent of Bulldog litters must now be delivered by Caesarian section since the pups' heads have become too big to be able to pass through their mothers' birth canals. Despite all the publicity that the chronic ailments of this breed has received, the popularity of the Bulldog has risen in the past decade.

The average life span of a Bulldog is now in the region of six years—less than half what many other breeds can expect. Indeed, researchers believe that the dogs have become so genetically similar to each other that it may prove impossible to breed healthier specimens from the existing stock. Fortunately, the Glen is not yet in a similar situation, but this is a crisis that could come to threaten a number of the rarer breeds. Obviously, the Glen's gene pool could be grown by systematic outcrossing. However, it might be inadvisable to cross with another dwarf breed since that could magnify genetic defects. On the other hand, if outcrossing occurs with non-dwarf breeds, that could undermine the distinctive nature of the Glen Terrier.

Today, there are still some Glen of Imaal terriers that fulfil the function for which they were first bred. However, the vast majority of Glens are now kept as family pets. They tend to be more even-tempered than most terriers, and of course they also bark a good deal less. They are intelligent, affectionate, loyal, and relate well to children. However, they have retained some of their former traits, including the hunting instinct. So, if you are taking your Glen Terrier for a quiet walk, and a small creature makes a sudden move in the bushes as you go past, it may well be their last.

In September of 2016 I attended a breed show for Glens in Moone in County Kildare, a small village best known for a High Cross that dates back over a thousand years to the ancient Celtic Church in Ireland. Although the procedure of exhibition and judging is standard in all shows, the feeling of this one was unusually relaxed and informal. It was the first time I had seen so many of this rare breed in one place, but it was still a small show, with fewer than thirty dogs competing, and not many more humans in attendance. It all seemed more like the gathering of an extended family than a competitive event. One of the dogs present was not even registered with the Irish Kennel Club, which would automatically disqualify him from any championship competition.

Dog breeding is now a huge global industry, and one that can prove highly lucrative for some breeders. They are sometimes presented as the exploiters of their hapless canine victims, and cynical operators who are driven purely by mercenary greed: the Gordon Gekkos, as it were, of the canine world. There were no breeders who had brought their dogs to Moone that day that looked to me as if they were making a lot of money from the trade in animals. None of those I met bred on a large scale, and their commitment to this type of terrier certainly did not appear to be due to financial calculation. In some cases they had been given a Glen, or had rescued one, or had been introduced to the breed by a friend. What they had in common was a degree of affection and commitment to the small dog that struck me as completely genuine.

In recent years there have been some signs of an increase in the popularity of the Glen Terrier, with breed clubs springing up in Holland, Sweden and Finland. Some have predicted that the Glen is set to become a new 'fad' breed, and one enthusiast has even claimed that 'with its compact size, easy-care coat and exceptional temperament and health, it is exactly what the American public seeks in a dog'. However, I think the Glen is unlikely, to say the least, to capitalise on the current vogue for miniature dogs that can be carried around in a handbag. This is a handsome, attractive and affectionate breed, but the adult dog does not display the childlike features of a dog like the Chihuahua. Having said that, I must admit that it can often prove hard to predict which dogs will fall in and out of fashion—as the history of another breed from Ireland amply demonstrates.

Whiptail: the Irish Water Spaniel

Although the provenance of the Irish Water Spaniel is Irish, the origins of the breed, like most of Ireland's native dogs, are clouded in obscurity. Some have claimed that the skeleton of a similar dog was excavated from some Roman remains dating from the first century AD. According to other reports, the roots of this spaniel can be traced back across three or four millennia to ancient Persia. There are more reliable descriptions of spaniels that resemble the current dog that date from almost a thousand years ago, but that connection is also speculative.

Five hundred years later, it was recorded that Queen Elizabeth I's spymaster, Sir Robert Cecil, gave a 'smooth-tailed' spaniel that came from Ireland to the King of France. A few years after that, the *Historie of the Four-Footed Beastes* described an Irish 'water spagnel' with long, rough, tightly curled hair, and there are also references from the sixteenth century to its 'bare and naked tail', which is still unique to the current breed, and which suggests that it may be its ancestor.

At one time, hawks or falcons were used to hunt waterfowl, and the function of spaniels was simply to 'spring' the birds from their cover. For many years, nets or bows and arrows were used to catch the game that had been flushed out by the dogs. However, during the course of the seventeenth century, the role of all spaniels, both land and water varieties, changed dramatically. The invention of flintlock weapons allowed dogs to be used more effectively for hunting wildfowl. Spaniels had previously been regarded as rather wild and undisciplined creatures; now they were transformed into well-trained and reliable gun dogs that could be used for wing shooting. It might be argued that the Irish Spaniel has managed to retain some of its original wildness: the dog has been described by Nick Waters as 'a bundle of rags in a cyclone', and has a well-founded reputation as an animal that craves excitement, and loves to hunt.

The Water Spaniel may be the oldest of Ireland's native breeds, and it is certainly the only Irish dog that can claim to have supernatural ancestors. The breed was once believed to be descended from the *dobhar-chú*. That name roughly translates from the Irish as 'water hound', but it can also simply mean 'otter', and this creature was supposed to be a mixture of both dog and otter, though it is also sometimes described as half-dog and half-fish. The *dobhar-chú* supposedly lived in loughs and isolated stretches of water in the west of Ireland. It was said to make a terrifying screeching sound when enraged, and sometimes attacked and killed human beings.

There is also the possibility that some of the ancestors of this spaniel were brought to Ireland by the 'pirate queen', Gráinne Ní Mháille. This formidable woman had inherited a large shipping business from her father, Eoghan Dubhdara

Ó Máille, and frequently visited Spain in the course of her eventful life. It is possible that she encountered Spanish water dogs on her travels and brought some of them back to Ireland—they bear a passing resemblance to the current Irish Water Spaniel.

Whether such a connection exists or not, this spaniel seems to have developed over time into two types, which were distinct in terms of colour and size. One was based in the north of Ireland, and the other in the south. The latter was described as a 'curly coated dog, with a low body, and long ears'. Its colouring was solid liver, with substantial feathering on its legs. The northern dogs are supposed to have been smaller, and to have had 'shorter ears, and a pointer-like face'. They were also liver coloured, but with white markings, and fewer feathers on their legs. J. S. Skidmore was an English field sports writer in the late nineteenth century who was regarded as a contemporary authority on the various breeds of gun dog, and he considered the northern spaniels to be 'third-rate specimens of their southern relations'.

The acknowledged founder of the modern breed was Justin McCarthy. He left no breeding records, which is not entirely surprising since he bred his dogs before detailed pedigrees had become well established. However, it appears that he used his kennels in Dublin in the early 1830s to bring the northern and southern spaniels together in a single breed. The spaniel he created seems to have taken much more of its genetic inheritance from the southern dog, but it has been suggested that McCarthy also outcrossed, perhaps with setters, to produce an improved version of the two basic types. It has even been proposed that the dog he produced, which was sometimes known as McCarthy's Spaniel, was not developed from an existing breed but was manufactured by McCarthy, and is, in effect, an early example of a 'designer-doodle' cross-breed.

It is also possible that McCarthy cross-bred with some water dogs from southern Europe, which he is known to have visited regularly. However, even a new type of dog needs some genetic material to build upon, and it seems very unlikely to me that McCarthy's breeding programme was not at least based upon the existing types of Irish Water Spaniel. There is also the matter of the trademark 'whiptail', which is unique to this one Irish dog and found nowhere else in the canine world. Perhaps even more critically, there is the fact that McCarthy managed to fix the breed type in just a few years, which seems an implausibly short period of time if he had been working more or less from scratch.

In 1859, McCarthy wrote a lengthy letter to *The Field* sporting magazine in which he outlined the standard points that he had followed in breeding his Irish Water Spaniels. He gave no information about the specimens that he had used in his programme, which has seemed curious to some, but he did outline in some detail the characteristics of the breed. What is remarkable about McCarthy's description of his Irish Water Spaniels is how many distinctive features he is able to list. It is also remarkable how little the current breed has diverged from his original type.

McCarthy was a keen sportsman, and no doubt his primary goal was simply to produce a superb water dog that could be used all over the island. He eventually bred a celebrated spaniel called Boatswain, which was also the name of Lord Byron's adored dog. McCarthy's spaniel was born in 1834, and lived for over eighteen years—an exceptionally long lifespan for any sort of dog in that period. During his lifetime, Boatswain sired many hunting and show dogs, and he is now accepted, in every sense, as the father of the Irish Water Spaniel breed. One of his sons, Jack, was born in 1849. He proved equal to his father in siring pups, and his name appears in many early pedigrees. By the early 1860s some dog shows were providing a special class for the Irish Water Spaniel, and in 1862 the spaniel appeared at the prestigious Birmingham show. Soon afterwards the breed was listed in the first English Stud Book.

The dog was described in detail by the naturalist A. E. Knox in 1857. He noted that the Irish spaniel had some obvious similarities in appearance to other breeds of water dog. The most obvious point of comparison is the Standard Poodle—in fact, the Irish dog looks rather like the Poodle's delinquent cousin. They are both scent dogs with a strong hunting instinct, and coats that are likely to cord if they are allowed to grow too long. However, it has also been suggested that the Irish spaniel is related to the Barbet, another French dog, and to the Portuguese and English Water Spaniels. It is unclear, however, whether the Irish dog might be an ancestor, descendant or mixture of those other breeds. What is clear is that the water spaniel has a number of its own singular features. They help to make this animal unique, and the Irish dog has even been described as 'the antipodes of any other of the varieties of spaniel'.

Water spaniels are the largest members of the spaniel group, which means that instead of going under cover when hunting, they can go through it and work at close range. The dog's physical type and size has led some to suggest that it should not be classified as a proper spaniel but as a retriever, and in fact it is only since the 1950s that it has been allowed to enter the spaniel class in dog shows. Its body can be described as 'cobby'—a term used by dog-breeders to indicate a compact frame. The Irish spaniel has a double coat, which consists of two layers of tight curls, which makes it waterproof. The dog's legs are well feathered, but it sheds very little, which means that this breed is also deemed suitable for those who suffer from allergies that are connected to dog hair.

The colour of the spaniel has remained solid liver, with a purple sheen that is not shared by any other breed. The Irish Water Spaniel also boasts a kind of topknot of long, loose curls that grow down from the head, and are often allowed to cover the eyes—which can give the animal a somewhat quizzical expression. The field sports writer J. S. Skidmore thought this made the dog look like 'a wild Irishman'. I think that the dog looks more like a drunken Irish set-dancer, or a follower of some canine Rastafarian cult. The dog's feet are webbed, like those of an otter hound. The face is entirely smooth and free of hair, and, unlike the poodle, this water dog does not need shaving or trimming to stay that way. One of the most distinctive features of the Irish Water Spaniel is its 'whiptail', which is hairless, except at the base, and which, in Skidmore's evocative words, 'tapers to a sting'.

This Irish spaniel is very well built, and its large, webbed feet also ensure that the dog is an exceptionally powerful swimmer. It was also bred by McCarthy to work differently in the field from conventional spaniels and retrievers. Until this dog appeared, spaniels had been used to flush out game, and retrievers, with their soft mouths, were called upon to carry the dead birds back without causing them any further damage.

McCarthy bred the Irish Water Spaniel to be multi-purpose. It was intended both to flush and retrieve snipe and wild fowl in Ireland's bogs, marshes and river estuaries. The dog was also bred to be fearless, if not reckless, and to plunge into water in almost any circumstances. J. S. Skidmore believed that the 'indomitable spirit' of the Irish dog would lead him into 'feats of daring from which many breeds would shrink'. He concluded that 'no sea is too rough, no pier too high, no water too cold' for this spaniel.

The dog's lively, bold and inquisitive nature, along with that slightly deranged expression, has sometimes led the spaniel to be described as the clown of Ireland's native breeds. When I was growing up, one of our neighbours owned a Water Spaniel. He always seemed to be getting into scrapes of some sort, and had acquired the local reputation of being quite mad, but in retrospect I think that reputation was not truly deserved, and the mischief and mayhem he seemed to create was largely a by-product of his excess energy. In reality, the Irish Water Spaniel possesses considerable intelligence, and is reckoned to display exceptional initiative and shrewd judgment when hunting. In general, this dog seems to have the knack of fulfilling even humdrum tasks in its own distinctive way. Perhaps that is why he appealed so strongly to two of Ireland's most-loved writers.

Amber Eyes

So far as I am aware, there is only one Irish Water Spaniel that features prominently in Irish fiction, and that is Maria, the memorable bitch that appears in Somerville and Ross's collections of short stories about an English Resident Magistrate (R.M.) working in rural Ireland at the end of the nineteenth century. When I was a teenager, my mother recommended that I read the R.M. stories, which she adored. However, I found that I disliked them, and I took an adolescent delight in drawing my mother's attention to what I considered to be their principal shortcomings.

It was not hard for me to find reasons for my dislike: it seemed obvious that the stories had been written with English and not Irish readers in mind, and they all appeared to follow the same predictable narrative. Above all, I was irritated by what seemed like a heavy reliance on quaint 'Irishisms'. These were usually hyperbolic expressions: 'the hair is after falling off me head, and the heart is scalded on me' sort of thing, which I presumed readers were supposed to find charming and amusing, but which left me distinctly unimpressed. It turns out that these phrases were reproduced faithfully from the notebooks that Edith Somerville carried around with her, and in which she jotted down any striking extravagance of speech that she overheard.

Some years later, I was asked to teach a University course on 'Anglo-Irish Literature', a term I detest, and I went back to the novels and stories that Somerville and Ross had written. I found to my surprise that they seemed to have improved greatly since I had last read them. Of course, the changes were in me. I should not have mocked my mother: her judgment proved to have been better than my own. The fiction these two women produced is not only extremely well written, it also provides a critical and penetrating insight into the twilight years of the southern Irish landed gentry. It was a world that they clearly knew inside out, and they wrote about it with a quiet but firm authority, along with a sense of critical distance. There are two other subjects to which they also bring an unmistakably informed knowledge: horses and dogs.

The central dynamic in the R.M. stories is generated between an English representative of the British administration in Ireland, who has some distant Irish connections, and a member of the local gentry and landowning classes. On one hand there is Major Yeates, a Resident Magistrate, who is portrayed as a well-meaning, but rather dull and literal-minded, official, who invariably fails to grasp the small but vital nuances of life in rural Ireland. On the other hand, there is Flurry Knox, a member of the Irish gentry and a fellow magistrate. Knox is driven by a kind of anarchic energy that verges at times on outright madness, but he also reveals a deep and intuitive understanding of his social environment. The relationship of Yeates and Knox is set against a backdrop of other Irish characters—eccentric landlords, stroppy servants, cunning farmers and assorted ne'er-do-wells—who are a source of bewilderment for Yeates, but entertain Knox. Maria, the

Irish Water Spaniel bitch, is one of the key players in this supporting cast.

The choice of a Water Spaniel in this context is significant in several respects. For obvious reasons, the breed was favoured in those counties in Ireland where there was an abundance of marshes, loughs and bogs—indeed, the spaniel was sometimes known as a 'bog-dog'. Although the Water Spaniel was often found in the homes of the hunting and shooting landowning classes, its owners tended to belong to the minor gentry. Writing in the 1870s, J. S. Skidmore commended the Water Spaniel to gentlemen of 'limited means', or those who 'have not the accommodation to keep a team of dogs', since the Irish breed could be trained 'to perform the duties of pointer, setter, retriever and spaniel'—a kind of canine one-stop shop.

In fact, ownership of the Irish Water Spaniel was not restricted to minor landowners. In a country that was regularly stricken by famine, wading birds and ducks could provide a source of food for an impoverished peasantry. The Water Spaniel was a hard-mouthed hunting dog that not only found game, but could catch and kill birds as well as retrieve them, which meant that ownership of expensive guns was not essential to the hunt. The unruly and excitable demeanour of this spaniel, and its apparently unkempt appearance, also meant that, unlike the Wolfhound or Red Setter, it was seldom praised for its aristocratic bearing, or for the dignified impression it created. At the same time, the historic roots of this spaniel in Ireland were indisputable, and so, whatever faults the dog may have had, they were home-grown.

In other words, part of Maria's role in these stories involves her capacity to span some of the different social, ethnic and political traditions within Ireland. In this, she may even reflect a balance in the different political perspectives of the two writers, Edith Somerville and Violet Martin (who wrote and was published under the name of 'Martin Ross'). They were cousins, but Martin was a committed Unionist, while Somerville came to sympathise with the cause of Irish Nationalism, and would often perform patriotic songs when called upon to sing at parties. (Sadly, her brother was murdered by the IRA at the family home in 1936.)

In other respects, the political views of both cousins were similar and progressive. They were convinced suffragettes, and active in the contemporary campaign to extend voting rights to women, with Martin acting as vice-president of the Munster Franchise League. As Declan Kiberd has argued, the R.M. stories link 'nostalgia for a dying way of life' with the subversive portrayal of a succession of 'strong and vital' female characters. One of these females is the formidable Lady Knox, another is Maria the Water Spaniel. Although Martin was friendly with leading figures in the Celtic Literary Revival such as Yeats (and can it be purely accidental that her myopic R.M. almost shares the same name?), Lady Gregory (to whom she was related) and Edward Martyn (to whom she was also related), both she and Somerville regarded the Celtic Revivalists' view of the Irish peasantry as excessively romantic and sentimental. To be fair, I think the cousins had a point.

One of my favourite passages in the R.M. stories that features Maria is narrated, as usual, by Major Yeates. He explains that the spaniel had been given to his wife as a wedding gift. She had hoped the bitch would grow to resemble the noble Irish Wolfhound Gelert (as described in Spencer's famous poem) and would prove to be 'a lamb at home, a lion in the chase'. It seems this was a forlorn hope. Yeates accepts that Maria has performed 'pretty well as a lion': she has chased 'all dogs unmistakably smaller than herself', and whenever possible has eaten the game that her master has shot. However, Major Yeates reckons that Maria has not proved very effective as a lamb: she has snatched 'cold beef from the luncheon table' and scratched 'the paint off the hall door' when she was banished for her crimes. She has also bitten beggars, bullied servants and hidden 'ducks' claws and fishes' backbones' behind the sofa cushions.

Despite all these transgressions, Yeates confesses that when Maria lays 'her brown snout' upon his knee, or rolls 'her blackguard amber eyes', or tries to smite him with 'her feather paw', he finds it impossible to remember her iniquities. When he prepares to go on a hunting expedition with the dog, Yeates admits that she ceases to be 'a buccaneer, a glutton and a hypocrite'. In fact, as soon as Maria realises that there is the possibility of a hunt, she cannot eat any breakfast due to her nerves, and waits in the hall, 'shivering with excitement' while 'agonising in her soul' that her master might leave without her.

Maria's insatiable appetite for hunting parallels that of Flurry Knox, who seems permanently to be dressed in riding gear, as if he were always ready to jump on his horse and lose himself in the delirium of the chase. However, the passage from which I have quoted reveals a genuine understanding and appreciation of the Irish Water Spaniel breed. It also expresses themes of exasperation, affection, and co-dependence that are connected to the ambivalent relations between a colonial power and Ireland's native population, which includes its gentry.

Once the type had been fixed by Justin McCarthy, the Irish Water Spaniel soon gained popularity with sportsmen and women in Ireland and beyond. It had been bred to work as part of a team, which made it easy to train, and it thrived on firm discipline. It was also valued for its energy, its courage, its powers of endurance and its ability to retrieve in rough and freezing water. J. S. Skidmore believed that the Irish Water Spaniel had 'no equal' for wildfowl retrieving, and that the dog embodied the 'purest of the pure-bred'. By the mid 1870s, the reputation of the breed had spread, and substantial numbers of Irish spaniels had been exported to Scandinavia and North America. Records show that in 1875 the Irish Water Spaniel was the third most popular sporting dog in the United States.

When the Irish Water Spaniel Club was founded in Dublin in 1890, the future of the breed seemed rosy and secure. But the popularity of the dog would peak in the early years of the following century. There were several reasons for the subsequent decline, and one of them was the emergence of an attractive rival breed. The origins of that dog lie in Newfoundland, in North America, but the breed was developed in England. A small group of wealthy British aristocrats collaborated over a period of almost half a century to establish the gun dog that became known as the Labrador Retriever. It seems their original intention was to keep the new breed reserved for themselves and a few select friends. However, that goal was eventually abandoned, and their dog was recognised by the British Kennel Club in 1903, and by the American Kennel Club in 1917. Like the Irish Water Spaniel, the Labrador Retriever could be used as a dual-purpose dog that could be worked on both land and water. Like the Irish Water Spaniel, the Labrador Retriever was able to retrieve even in the worst conditions.

However, the Labrador had other features that made it desirable both as a hunting and as a family dog, and which gave it wider appeal than the Water Spaniel. To begin with, the Labrador Retriever had a short, smooth coat that was easier to groom than that of the Irish dog. It was more even-tempered and patient than the high-spirited spaniel, which meant that it could make the transition from being a hunting dog to becoming a family pet with greater ease. Unlike the Water Spaniel, the Labrador had a soft mouth, which reinforced a sense of its gentle nature, and made it a more useful retriever. It was also available in a variety of colours. Although it was originally liver-coloured (and yellow pups were once culled at birth), by the end of the nineteenth century the blond or yellow version had become very popular, and a black Labrador was bred in the 1930s. These three principal colours have become associated with different roles. The yellow Labrador often works as a service dog; the black as a gun dog; and the liver version as a show dog.

It seems small wonder that this retriever is currently listed by the American Kennel Club as the most popular dog breed in the United States, as it has been for more than twenty-five years, while the Irish Water Spaniel languishes in 149th position, perilously close to the bottom of the table. The appeal of the Labrador crosses many boundaries: it is the most owned and registered breed of dog in the world, and it seems unrealistic to expect the Irish Water Spaniel to compete in those popularity stakes. But this Irish dog has always been something of an outsider, and it would appear that its strengths are not in keeping with the times in which we live. Its appearance would not usually be described as 'cute', and it could never function as any sort of lapdog. It can look a little strange, and its character has even been described as 'wild and wayward'. Nowadays, the Irish Water Spaniel is rarely seen, even in its ancestral homeland.

But this is a breed that combines acute intelligence and raw courage with a simple *joie de vivre*. It is not aggressive, and is acutely sensitive to human emotions. There was a time when those qualities were highly prized in a dog. They were certainly respected and valued by Somerville and Ross. And, for those who can appreciate such virtues, the Irish Water Spaniel is still your only man. But it is not the only Irish dog whose popularity seems to have peaked many years ago.

Daredevil: the Irish Terrier

Some have claimed that the Irish Terrier is the oldest breed of its type in Ireland. William Haynes, an early admirer, believed it was 'probable' that the dog was of ancient origin, but admitted that there was not 'one scrap of direct documentary evidence' to prove or justify his claim. Herbert Compton, another admirer of the breed, writing in 1903, was more candid. He described the dog as a 'product of civilisation' rather than nature, and accepted that the current breed had only been 'gradually and skilfully developed' in recent years. The same writer maintained that this terrier was still 'as Irish as the Shamrock', though he conceded that it was likely that the breed now included 'a dash of the Scotch blood [that] you find in Protestant Ulster'. That might explain the somewhat forceful and single-minded nature of this breed.

Like most Irish dogs, there seems to have been a great variation in the size, shape and colour of the terrier before selective breeding was properly introduced in the 1880s. This was demonstrated at the Exhibition Palace Show in Dublin in 1873, when there were two separate classes for Irish Terriers: one for those who weighed over nine pounds, and one for those under that weight. Writing thirty years later, one breeder recalled the 'medley of types' from which the modern terrier had evolved, and the 'uncompromisingly divergent specimens' of the breed that were seen in the early days of its exhibition.

In the case of the Irish Terrier, we can identify two specific dogs who might fairly be regarded as having provided the foundation for the current breed. Killiney Boy and Erin were first shown in the late 1870s, and Killiney Boy is listed in no less than twenty-eight separate pedigrees as the sire, while Erin appears in twenty-five as the dam. Killiney Boy was described by William Haynes as a 'small dog, low on the leg and inclined to be too cobby', which means that he was of a compact shape. Erin, whom Haynes identified as 'the mother of the breed', was also small, 'with cropped ears, fine legs and feet', but 'all Irish from tip to toe'.

At that time the colour of the breed had not been settled, and apart from various shades of red (golden, dark and wheaten), there were also black and tan and brindled dogs. It is believed that the defining red coat came from one of Killiney Boy and Erin's numerous offspring: a bitch called Poppy, who was born bright red (hence the name), and who threw a sizeable number of pups that were the same colour. The Irish dog is still the only all-red terrier breed, but for many years litters would contain some pups that were of a different colour, and these were rigorously culled.

According to one historian of the breed, there was 'a large strain' of Irish Terriers in County Cork, which were mostly wheaten coloured. However, the breed's main stronghold was in County Antrim in the north of Ireland. These dogs were described as 'racy in type', with 'long punishing jaws' and a 'soft and open coat'. It was this northern strain that seems to have provided the basis for the modern Irish Terrier. Much of the credit for the establishment of the show standard must go to a breeder from Newtownbreda (then a small village to the south-east of Belfast) called William Graham. He was the owner of Erin, the founding dam of the modern breed. Graham devoted most of his adult life to the promotion of Irish Terriers, and attended so many dog shows outside Ireland that he eventually became known as 'the Irish Ambassador'. The succession of purebreds that passed through his kennels have featured in the pedigrees of many future generations.

The breed standards that Graham helped to set for the Irish Terrier were sometimes summed up by the three R's: racy, red and rectangular. The dog was bred by him to be fast-paced, lithe and powerful, with a lean, taut and balanced frame. Graham used close inbreeding and culling to establish a strain with a smart red coat and a relatively long head. It has been suggested that he outcrossed with Welsh and English dogs to produce the rapid changes that were needed to develop a more streamlined outline. Whatever the truth of that, Graham clearly intended to distinguish the Irish Terrier from its relatives. Its body was proportionately longer than its Kerry Blue or Wheaten cousins, and so were its legs. Its broken coat was dense, tight and wiry, never 'soft, silky, curly, wavy or woolly'. And, as one breeder observed, this terrier's expression, 'like its nature', was intense. The overall appearance is rather similar to that pursued by William Graham's namesake, Captain Graham, in his breeding programme for Wolfhounds, although, obviously, the Irish Terriers were designed on a much smaller scale. That might explain why some commentators, such as William Haynes, were led to speculate that the two dogs might be related, but, so far at least, there is no firm evidence of that.

The terrier's coat was cut for show in a highly stylised fashion that emphasised the clean lines of its physique. At first it was also the custom to dock the dog's tail to about two-thirds of its original length. It was also common to crop the terrier's ears. However, when the Irish Terrier Club was formed in 1879, Graham helped to introduce a rule that forbade ear-cropping. This proved both popular and effective—so much so that the Kennel Club in Great Britain soon ruled that no Irish Terrier whose ears had been cropped would be allowed to compete in a recognised breed show. This led, ultimately, to the Kennel Club banning the ear-cropping of all breeds. Nowadays, the Irish Terrier's ears are small, and are supposed to fold forward, just above the top of its head. However, in order to achieve that effect, terrier pups may need to have their ears trained, and this is usually done by gluing them to their head for up to seven or eight months. This process does not always prove successful, and there have been rumours that some owners have resorted to surgical procedures to attain the desired result.

The Irish Terrier standard was drawn up in 1879, and from the start the dog proved to have widespread popular appeal. It was hailed as the perfect all-round dog: 'the poor man's sentinel, the farmer's friend, and the gentleman's favourite', which suggests an unusual ability to transcend social divisions in Ireland. It also became the first member of the terrier group to be recognised by the British Kennel Club as a native Irish breed. By the end of the 1880s, Irish Terriers were one of the most popular dogs in Great Britain as well as Ireland. Their appeal seemed to span many social classes, and in the years leading up to World War One the breed had become even more fashionable, with very large sums of money being paid for outstanding specimens.

These terriers could often be found in the royal palaces of Europe and beyond. The Habsburgs used them as shooting dogs, and the Rajahs and Maharajahs of British India were also fond of the breed—indeed, a painting of one still hangs in Delhi's government buildings. The Irish Terrier Association was formed in England in 1911, and the first president was the Marquis of Breadalbane, while its vice presidents included H. H. the Maharajah of Jind, The Lord Dewar, and Maj. Gen. Sir Foster Newline. When King Edward VII paid a state visit to Ireland in 1903, he brought his Irish Terrier, Jack, with him. Unfortunately, Jack died soon after their arrival. He was buried with due ceremony in the garden of what was then the vice-regal lodge in Dublin's Phoenix Park, where a small white marble headstone is still dedicated to 'King Edward's favourite Irish Terrier, who only lived twelve hours after reaching his native land.'

By then, the Irish Terrier had become popular in North America. The first time that the breed was shown there was in 1880. Then, in 1887, two of William Graham's young dogs were sent to a breeder in Philadelphia, where they made a considerable impact. The first Irish Terrier was exhibited at the Westminster show in 1881, and the breed was officially recognised by the American Kennel Club in 1885. A few years later, more of Graham's stock arrived in Philadelphia, and this laid the basis for the future development of the Irish dog in the United States. The Irish Terrier Club of America was founded in 1896, and its aim was to promote the pure breeding of what its members thought was 'just about the most satisfying terrier extant'.

The dog had already acquired the nickname of 'Daredevil' because of its audacious character. According to one patronising English writer, Ireland had always been famous for 'its women, its horses, and its dogs'. He believed that the Irish peasantry 'gave little heed to appearance—only to courage', and because the Irish terrier 'retained and accentuated that characteristic', he judged that it had fully earned its nickname. The dog also enjoyed a reputation for its intelligence, grit and initiative. William Graham once remarked that there was no need for Noah to take a pair of Irish Terriers on board his Ark because 'they could swim alongside so well'. In both the UK and the United States, the breed became associated with characteristics that were considered to be typically Irish, such as its 'fire and animation' and its 'heedless, reckless pluck', which could, on occasion, be 'blind to all consequences'.

This reputation was enhanced by the courage and loyalty shown by an Irish terrier called Wee Jock during the Eureka rebellion in Australia, when a group of gold miners engaged in an armed confrontation with British troops. It is reckoned that thirty miners were killed during the brief skirmish that took place at their stockade in 1854, and many of those who died were Irish. Among them was Wee Jock's master. The dog guarded his body fiercely during the following hours, and later accompanied the death cart that transferred the corpse to a cemetery. It is said that Wee Jock howled like a banshee all the while. In 1997, the dog was awarded the Purple Cross, the RSPCA's highest award for bravery, and a handsome bronze statue of the terrier now stands at the site of the stockade.

Perhaps the story of Wee Jock appealed to the American writer Jack London. He had achieved worldwide fame with two novels, *The Call of the Wild* and *White Fang*, in which the central characters were feral dogs and wolves. London used these animals to explore the existential themes of survival, and he drew upon his own testing experiences during the Klondike Gold Rush. He claimed that one of his last novels, *Jerry of the Islands*, was also based on his real-life experiences. In this case, it involved his search in the South Pacific for the remains of some friends, whom, he alleged, had been killed and eaten by cannibals, though some have disputed the accuracy of his claim.

During his time in the South Seas, he and his wife had encountered an Irish Terrier bitch called Peggy, to whom they became so attached that they stole the dog and kept her. Perhaps in London's mind the Irish Terrier was as near to a feral animal as any purebred and domesticated dog could get. At any rate, for Jerry, the terrier in his novel and its central character, the word 'master' simply does not exist. That is apparently because he is as proud and headstrong an animal as his Irish ancestry suggests. Sadly, the novel is of a markedly inferior quality to London's earlier novels— all too characteristic of his later writing—and he may be one of those authors who draw inspiration from their earlier novels, and can be fairly accused of plagiarising their own work. This book and its sequel are also marred by the explicit racism of their author, whose obnoxious views are evidently shared by his dog-hero, Jerry.

London wrote this novel during World War One—an event that was to change popular perceptions of the Irish Terrier because of the role the dog played in that dreadful conflict.

True Grit

When hostilities broke out in 1914, there was just one single dog, apart from a few regimental pets and mascots, serving in the entire British Army. However, one former officer, Colonel Edwin Richardson, had been convinced for some time of the active role that he believed dogs could play in modern warfare. He had even noticed that German officers came to England to buy specimens of dogs that were intended for future military use in Germany. When he retired from the army, Richardson and his wife had established a kennel in Scotland, where they trained their own dogs for the same purpose. In August 1914, he offered their services, and some ambulance dogs that he had trained, to the British Red Cross. Unfortunately, it soon became clear that such dogs could not be used very effectively in a war zone since they were often shot before they could be of any practical assistance to wounded soldiers.

Richardson decided to train dogs for sentry duty, but he also began to see the potential of a more active part that certain breeds could play as messengers in the front line of the trenches. Until then, most messages between military posts were carried manually by soldiers, and the attrition rate was high. Richardson took dogs to artillery batteries so that they would become used to the sound of gunfire, and he taught them to connect that sound with food so that they would want to deliver their messages as quickly as possible to receive a reward. In 1916 he provided the first two Airedale Terriers to carry messages between forward and command posts on the Western Front. It soon became clear that the experiment had proved very successful: Richardson's dogs were faster and more agile than human messengers, which made them more difficult for the enemy to identify and kill. In 1917, Richardson was asked by the British War Office to establish a War Dog School—which still exists, though now it is home to the Military Dog Training Regiment.

There was an urgent demand for these dogs during World War One. At first they were obtained from the Home for Lost Dogs at Battersea in London, and other dogs' homes in British cities were also informed that their animals were needed for active service in Flanders. Stray dogs were rounded up by the police, but even that was not enough, and appeals were made to the general public to surrender their pets. This was obviously a dangerous role for domestic animals, but the response was overwhelming. One woman wrote to Richardson: 'I have given my husband and my sons, and now that he too is required, I give my dog.' Apart from carrying messages, dogs were also employed as scouts, using their sense of smell to locate enemy troops up to 1,000 metres away. They were trained not to bark, but only to give a low growl, raise their hackles and point. By the end of the war, messenger and scout dogs were assigned as a matter of routine to most battalions in the front line, and more than 20,000 dogs had served in the Allied forces, with even more used by the Central Powers of Germany and Austria-Hungary.

Despite the strong public response, not all the animals that were sent to be trained were considered suitable for service. Richardson had firmly held reservations about some of the breeds he was offered. He thought that fox terriers, for example, were too fond of play to be reliable, and that retrievers would prove too compliant to show initiative in difficult situations. However, Richardson believed that Irish Terriers were well suited to the demands of the job, and he began to recruit them in substantial numbers. He even claimed to believe that these dogs understood the importance of their work, and felt 'highly honoured' to be employed as 'servants of His Majesty'. He believed that they were all much happier serving the Empire than merely 'loafing around' at home. In general, he regarded Irish Terriers as 'highly sensitive, spirited dogs', who displayed the 'finer qualities of mind' and were 'extraordinarily intelligent, faithful and honest'. According to Richardson, 'many a soldier' had survived the war because of the Irish Terrier.

Apart from the many individual acts of bravery they performed, these 'soldier-dogs' were also extremely popular with the ordinary troops—who christened them the 'Micks', and with whom they lived and died. The Irish Terriers proved cheerful companions, who helped to sustain morale in grim circumstances. They were also enthusiastic ratters, killing many of the vermin that infested the trenches and feasted on the plentiful supply of bodies in no-man's land. The terriers received a bowl of biscuits every morning, which was usually enough to fuel them for the whole day. One of the best-known of these Irish dogs had the unlikely name of Goldberg. This terrier was brought to France with the 122nd Field Artillery Regiment of the US Army. He was gassed on the Western Front, and also severely wounded by shrapnel. This led to his honourable discharge, but he was held in such high regard that, when he died, his body was sent to a taxidermist to be preserved. His remains may currently be found in the Illinois State Military Museum.

Sadly, a large number of these dogs never made it back to their homes in Ireland or elsewhere, and many suffered horrific injuries from bullets, bombs, and mustard gas, with some even displaying the symptoms of what is now termed post-traumatic stress disorder. However, the British popular press soon found a story that seemed to exemplify the loyalty and fighting spirit of the Irish dog—with the clear inference that this reflected the same qualities found in the tens of thousands of Irish soldiers who were then serving with the British Army in France, Belgium or Mesopotamia.

Prince was the name of an Irish Terrier who was alleged to have made his way to the British trenches in order to be reunited with his master. It seems that Private James Brown had left his dog with his wife in Buttevant, County Cork, when he was sent to France. The terrier was inconsolable at Brown's departure, and disappeared one day soon afterwards. However, two weeks after Prince had disappeared, Brown informed his wife that the dog had arrived safely with him in Armentières. There was never any explanation of how he had managed to get there, but the British press picked up the story, and ran with it periodically for the remainder of the war. It all seems highly implausible to me, but the RSPCA investigated the case after the war, and reported that it was true: somehow, Prince had managed to reach his master in the trenches.

Brown's regiment adopted Prince as a mascot, and he was given a small khaki jacket and his own identification dog-tag.

He was even provided with a miniature gas mask. According to the British newspapers, Prince amused the troops by being able to balance a penny on his nose, and catch it when the name of their regiment was called out. It was also claimed that he was a superb ratter who once killed 137 vermin in a single day. At one stage of the war there were so many dogs in the trenches that an order was issued from general headquarters that some of them had to be shot, but Prince managed to dodge that and every other bullet. Unlike so many of the soldiers whom he befriended, entertained and distracted, he survived the carnage and returned home in 1919.

Ireland had become a very different country in the years that followed World War One to the one that Prince and the Irish troops had left. In the aftermath of the Easter Rising in 1916, and the subsequent executions by the British of its leaders, a wave of intense Nationalist sentiment had swept over much of the island. The soldiers who had answered the call of the Irish Nationalist leader John Redmond and enlisted in Irish regiments of the British Army were not uniformly welcomed back to Ireland as heroes. Instead, they returned to a country that was about to embark on a War of Independence and a harsh campaign of attrition waged against some of their former comrades.

In that context, many of those who had fought for the British in World War One found it expedient to keep a low profile, and not to draw attention to their service records, since it seemed that Nationalist Ireland had come to regret its part in the war. The strong identification of the Irish Terrier with the British Army had also become something of a liability in many parts of Ireland. This was the political background in which the popularity of the Kerry Blue Terrier started to rise, while that of its cousin, the Irish Terrier, began a corresponding decline. There is not a simple equation at work here, but it is only in relatively recent years that the involvement of more than 200,000 Irish soldiers in World War One has been fully accepted and openly acknowledged in their own country.

The Irish Terriers' sacrifices in that war have also been marked in England. The Animal War Memorial on London's Park Lane includes a frieze carved into the wall that depicts the menagerie of animals—cats, elephants, camels—that served with the British Armed Forces. Included among them is the unmistakable profile of an Irish Terrier. As James Jackson, writing in *Country Life*, has observed, its ears are cocked and the dog is 'alert, quizzical and resolutely facing forward'.

In England, the end of the war was followed by a brief surge in the popularity of the Irish Terrier, with a record number of over a thousand pups registered in 1923 alone. Perhaps that had been fuelled by a late burst of patriotic feeling, but the mood in the United Kingdom was also shifting, and this was reflected in changing attitudes towards the terrier. Perhaps the dog was too strongly associated with a war that people simply wanted to forget. There might even have been some feelings of guilt at the amount of suffering that had been inflicted by human beings on an innocent species.

The subsequent decline in the popularity of the terrier may also have been caused, in part, by the long-term impact of breeding restrictions imposed during the war, as well as by a simple desire on the part of the dog-owning public for a change of fashion. As the 1920s progressed, other smaller and perhaps less-demanding breeds, such as the Pekinese and the Cocker Spaniel, seemed more appealing, and perhaps more in tune with a new spirit of transience and deliberate frivolity.

Whatever the cause, the numbers of Irish Terriers registered in England began to fall away during the inter-war years.

This reduction in the popularity of the terrier was not confined to Ireland and Great Britain, and nor was it restricted to one breed. The appeal of all types of terrier seemed to reach a peak in the mid 1920s, and since then most of them have experienced a protracted decline. Oliver Roeder had identified some of the possible causes for this development, which range from the devastating impact of the Wall Street Crash in 1929 on the American pedigree dog market to the difficulties and demands involved in grooming and maintaining some of the terrier breeds. The preferred method of grooming an Irish Terrier is known as 'stripping', and since these dogs don't shed, this entails using one's hands, or a dull knife, to remove any dead hair from the dog's outer coat, which can sometimes prove to be a laborious and time-consuming chore.

Apart from such practical considerations, it is clear that the fashions and tastes that had made terriers so popular in the first quarter of the last century, have changed. The Irish dogs belong to a strong-willed and intelligent breed, and, like most other terriers, they demand and need an active engagement with their owners. That level of commitment is not to everyone's liking, which may also help to explain why these types of dog are seen so seldom nowadays. The Airedale, Wire Fox, Scottish and Sealyham Terriers were once to be observed in the company of the rich and famous, with owners such as King George V, Cary Grant and Elizabeth Taylor. Now, some of those breeds are closer to extinction than the Bengal Tiger.

According to the latest figures, fewer than 300 new Irish Terriers were registered in 2015 in the United States—in the same period, more than 60,000 Golden Retriever pups were born. The proportions are somewhat similar in the UK. But although these are small numbers for the Irish dog, they seem just about enough to maintain the breed's healthy existence. There may no longer be large-scale kennels in Ireland, Great Britain and the United States that are producing sizeable numbers of these terriers, however there are some signs that indicate the Irish dog is making something of a comeback as a family pet, particularly with those families that own a substantial garden.

In appearance, these dogs have changed little since William Graham first bred the modern Irish Terrier in the 1870s. They are, perhaps, a little longer in the leg, and their ears may be carried somewhat higher, than in his original breed. They are also reckoned to be rather more biddable nowadays, and they often feature in obedience and agility competitions. These changes are significant, but it may be more important to recognise that, according to one breeder, 'the flame in their eyes is still the same'. These are healthy and extrovert animals, and their courage, initiative and sociability have remained intact since the breed was first fixed. There are now ambitious breeding programmes for these terriers in several countries, and the price of their pups has risen significantly in recent years. I would like to regard that as a sign that there is still life left in the old dog.

At one stage the Irish Terrier may have fallen out of favour with Irish Nationalists, but at least there were no concerted attempts to poison this dog. The same cannot be said for another of Ireland's native breeds.

The Sweetest Music:
the Kerry Beagle

The Kerry Beagle may seem like a dog of contradictions. Despite its name, this hound is generally not considered to be a beagle. It is leaner, more muscular and almost twice the size of the standard beagle. Many doubt that they are even related. Neither is it certain that this type of hound originated in County Kerry, though it has a strong association with the south-west of Ireland. While the dog is thought by some to be the oldest of all of Ireland's native breeds, it is still not recognised by the American Kennel Club, or by the Fédération Cynologique Internationale. In fact, with the notable exception of Ireland, there is no major kennel club anywhere in the world that recognises this dog as a distinct breed. Ironically, the Kerry Beagle is believed to be one of the dogs that contributed to the creation of the American Foxhound and various types of Coonhound, which are now recognised by the American and other national kennel clubs.

Like all of Ireland's native dogs, the origins of the Kerry Beagle are not clear or agreed, and they have also generated their own myths and legends. Some of these feature themes that occur in the creation stories of other breeds. However, there is one original and appealing story of how the dog is supposed to have arrived in Ireland. It was said that when Noah's ark rested briefly against the peak of Galtymore (the highest mountain in County Tipperary), two black-and-tan hounds caught the scent of a fox, and jumped ship to chase it. They were never seen again, and Noah had to proceed on his way without them. Others have claimed that the dog is descended from the Southern Hound, or from the Celtic dogs featured in the ancient sagas. However, since both those breeds are long gone, it is impossible to verify either claim.

Perhaps inevitably, there are also stories that connect the Kerry Beagle with a shipwrecked galleon from the Spanish Armada, and a dog that managed to swim ashore. Other stories claim that these animals arrived from France with Spanish traders in the seventeenth century, or were brought from continental Europe by descendants of the 'Wild Geese' who had joined the French Army. Some have noted similarities in markings and vocal range between the Irish dog and the Ariege Hound from south-west France, and there have been claims that outcrossing with that breed has taken place from time to time over the past few centuries. It also seems likely that some of the current Kerry Beagle's ancestors were foxhounds or harriers that had been imported from England, and were used for hunting by the Irish gentry. It is possible that they were mated with other dogs that were already in Ireland, and this helped to produce a new breed.

What is certain is that the Kerry Beagle is a pack animal, and Ireland's only native scent hound. Like most such hounds, these hunting dogs have long, drooping ears. Some have suggested that this trait helps them to collect scent from the air, as their ears swing back and forwards and direct it to the dog's nose. This seems unlikely to me, but their acute receptivity to smell is certainly increased by their large nasal cavities. They are also known for their 'hare foot', with the middle toe longer than the rest. This is supposed to afford them greater endurance on rough and broken ground, and contrasts with the 'catlike' foot of the English Foxhound.

In 1851, H. D. Richardson, the dog-breeder and Wolfhound enthusiast, described the dog as a 'fine, tall and dashing hound' with 'deep chops' and 'broad, pendulous ears'. He compared the Kerry Beagle in appearance and colouring to the Bloodhound. Twenty-five years later, Hugh Dalziel also thought the dog looked like 'a miniature Bloodhound', with many of 'that noble dog's chief characteristics'. For me, the resemblance is a little closer to a foxhound, though the Irish dogs are somewhat longer in the face, and are also held to be straighter in the hind leg. Their heads are more conical, and have an occipital bone on the top. Originally, the Irish hound was used to hunt stags and other substantial game. At first, it seems the Kerry Beagle worked in conjunction with a larger hunting dog: the smaller hound used its highly developed sense of smell to track the quarry, while the larger dog, probably a Wolfhound, would catch and kill the game. This offers one possible explanation for the puzzling name of the Kerry Beagle—the Irish word *beag* means 'small'.

Kerry Beagles are distinct from other types of scent hounds in both their temperament and their particular hunting technique. A pack of Kerry Beagles will usually fan out in a circular shape when hunting, but will always turn to the first hound that finds the scent, and indicates it by 'opening' with a loud bay. When the quarry is found, the pack re-forms and works collectively. Individual dogs usually take the same position in the pack every time they hunt. Whether one approves of hunting or not, it can still prove exhilarating to witness a pack of hounds in full cry. According to one admirer, 'nothing is more beautiful than to watch a really even pack turning in its tracks', without a single straggler 'to spoil the perfection of the movement'. Thady Ryan, a Master of the famous Scarteen Hunt, believed that 'on a good scenting day' the pack works like an orchestra, with all of the dogs 'beamed on one wavelength'.

The Kerry Beagles are also noted for bursts of great speed, and that can be very demanding of the hunters who are following them. Their baying is called 'music', and its deep, long notes can echo for miles through the Irish countryside. This is not only an attractive and evocative sound to hear—'rich and wonderfully sweet', according to David Hancock—the confidence of the whole pack also appears to improve when they are 'speaking' to each other, and their cries provide a kind of soundtrack and canine commentary on the nature and stage of the chase. It can also prove of practical benefit since it allows hunters to follow the pack of dogs when they are obscured by trees or cover.

The Kerry Beagles are generally rated as a hunting dog of the first order, with a long and respected history. In 1834, it seems that a test run was arranged between the Irish breed and English Foxhounds, and the Irish dogs won convincingly: they were faster over ditches and banks than the foxhounds, and were reckoned to have more sensitive noses. The Scarteen pack has even earned a place in the *Guinness Book of Records* for an epic hunt that covered more than twenty miles.

Hunting as a sport was extremely popular in rural Ireland for much of the nineteenth century. Its popularity was not confined to landowners, but they provided its core following and support for most of that century. Hunting had a special significance for the Irish gentry, particularly in the west of

Ireland, where they often lived considerable distances apart and could feel isolated and vulnerable. Perhaps the wildness and excitement of a hunt distracted members of the landowning classes, and allowed them to forget—at least temporarily— the growing threat to their privileged social position. The hunting season usually began in November and ended in March. It was an activity that could be pursued by both male and female members of the gentry, which encouraged their sense of social cohesion and political solidarity. The hunting season culminated in the annual Hunt Ball, where romantic liaisons could also be formed. This is a social institution that is, of course, still in existence, though the composition of those attending has changed greatly.

According to Declan Kiberd, the hunt came to represent 'the sovereignty of an upper class', and hunting not only helped to clear their land of foxes, it also served to remind their tenants 'who the rulers of that land really were'. Brendan Behan memorably defined the typical 'Anglo-Irishman' as a 'Protestant on a horse'. George Bernard Shaw thought that hunting epitomised the intellectual bankruptcy of the Irish landowning class since it may have produced 'hardy bodies' but only 'timid souls'. He believed the Irish gentry could talk ad nauseam about the broken limbs they had sustained in the chase, but were not able to come up with any original conversation or provocative ideas. That might seem both unfair and ungracious on Shaw's part. He had, after all, enjoyed the hospitality of Lady Gregory, a playwright, translator and theatrical innovator, whose family, the Persses, were well known (if not notorious) for their love of the chase. Shaw would also have been aware of the sophisticated fiction of Somerville and Ross, who were both positively addicted to hunting, and regularly rode to hounds (on side-saddle).

And Shaw lived long enough to have read the provocative and mildly risqué novels of Molly Keane, who claimed she only wrote to finance her passion for the sport.

A pack is counted in twos, or 'couples', and in the early years of the nineteenth century there could be packs of up to 100 couples, or 200 hounds. Many of these substantial packs were broken up during and after the Great Famine of the 1840s, when, in the words of Rawdon Lee, who was then editor of *The Field*, the Irish gentry were 'almost ruined'. They may not have starved, but many were forced to sell off their precious family domains. Nonetheless, it is hard to feel much sympathy for the landlord in Kilkenny who complained about how much distress he experienced when he saw starving peasants as he rode out, and yet still felt a prior obligation to feed his hounds. It may seem extraordinary that hunting continued even during the Famine, and that packs of dogs were fed while human families starved. It is, however, not surprising that this generated a great deal of understandable and long-lasting resentment among those suffering from hunger and deprivation. During 'Black 47', the worst year of the Famine, the *Limerick Reporter*, a Nationalist newspaper, drew attention to the 'terrible discordance' between the sound of 'the huntsman's horn, and the yelping pack' and the 'groans of the dying parent and the cries of children perishing for the lack of food'.

Four decades later, some of the descendants of those who starved during the Great Famine were able to exact a kind of revenge for the indifference of some landlords to the plight of their tenants. However, it was not only the Irish gentry who suffered from such reprisals; it was also their dogs, some of whom were to pay with their lives.

Stopping the Hunt

Despite the bankruptcy that many landlords faced as a result of the Famine, when the Irish Masters Fox Hunting Association was formed in 1859, a fair number of landowning families were still able to keep their own packs, and, as well as foxhounds and harriers, many if not most of these were Kerry Beagles. The dogs were bred to hunt, and were seldom exhibited in shows. While pedigrees were kept, these hounds were judged primarily by their physical abilities, by their noses, their courage and their stamina, and not by their physical appearance. However, in the early 1880s, the Kerry Beagle became one of the few breeds of dog to have been killed deliberately for political reasons.

A campaign had been launched by the National Land League to prevent landlords and magistrates from hunting across tenanted land. This combined political, social and economic grievances in a concerted challenge to one of the landlords' most treasured rituals. The campaign was part of a wider agitation for land reform in Ireland (the so-called 'Land War'), and many hunts felt compelled to quit the field when they were confronted by large and angry crowds carrying pikes, scythes and assorted cudgels. Masters of hunts who refused to back down ran the risk of losing their hounds through poisoning. Indeed, so much poisoned meat was laid across the roads and fields used by hunts that riders began to carry emetics to give their dogs in case they became ill.

On other occasions, hounds were found with their throats cut, and farmers were threatened with death if they allowed hunts to cross their land. Some of the gentry could not conceive that this opposition had originated with their own tenants. Some, like Edmund Dease, a member of the Westmeath Hunt, preferred to believe that it had all been caused by 'cowardly politicians who sent down organised mobs to stop the hunt'. Others, like Harry Sergent, writing for *The Field* under the pseudonym of 'The Fox', protested that 'hunting is a sport pure and simple', which everyone had an 'equal right to enjoy'. However, to adapt Oscar Wilde's dictum, sport is rarely pure, and never simple.

By January of 1882, many hunts had suspended their activities indefinitely, and some had announced that they were selling off their packs. The movement to stop hunts in Ireland was not a protest against hunting per se: in fact, the protesters sometimes formed their own 'national' packs, and large numbers of farmers and agricultural labourers would gather near a covert or wood with their farm or domestic dogs, and openly poach game on their landlord's grounds. Harry Sergent, aka 'The Fox', could not resist commenting on the disparate nature of the dogs assembled for one of these hunts, claiming with heavy irony that there was 'none of that monotonous black and tan' colouring in the pack he had seen. Instead, he noted, the dogs were of 'all sizes, races and ages'. They may even have included a few pedigree hounds, he conceded, but these were 'probably purloined' from their rightful owners.

Eventually, the campaign against fox-hunting ended. It had contributed to the British government's decision to release Charles Stewart Parnell, the leader of the Irish Nationalist Home Rule League at Westminster, and Michael Davitt, the leader of the Land League, from Kilmainham Gaol, where they had been imprisoned for allegedly promoting agrarian violence. Their freedom was contingent on a renunciation of extra-parliamentary activity. Following his release, Parnell founded the Irish Parliamentary Party, which was pledged to exclusively democratic and peaceful protests. In that context, there was an obvious incentive to call off the large-scale disruption of Irish hunts.

There was already a sense of fatigue among some of the protestors, and police containment of the demonstrations was proving more effective. By the end of the 1880s, hunting had largely resumed, but the campaign to stop the hunts had achieved much of its underlying purpose. A powerful blow had been dealt to the morale of the landed gentry. They were, as historian L. P. Curtis has commented, largely 'Church of Ireland, as well as landed'. Even though the landed gentry only constituted a small fraction of Ireland's Protestant population, the blow to their morale still had a sectarian dimension, and was felt by the wider Protestant community.

In fact, hunting had never appealed only to one denomination of the Irish gentry. Daniel O'Connell, the Nationalist leader who helped to secure Catholic Emancipation, is said to have been 'passionately attached' to the sport of hunting with his pack of Kerry Beagles. He had inherited the dogs from his uncle, Maurice 'Hunting Cap' O'Connell, who seemed, as his name suggests, to be obsessed with the chase, and the Liberator claimed that 'the sweetest music in the world' was the cry of his hounds. O'Connell is also said to have remarked that his pack had 'the dignity and presence' of the Lord Chancellor of England, with 'tenfold of his honesty'. However, even O'Connell's family were to not immune to the financial exigencies of maintaining a large pack of hounds. In 1870, Sir Maurice O'Connell, his nephew, reluctantly felt compelled to get rid of the pack of Kerry Beagles that had been kept by the family for many generations.

There are records of other family packs in Kerry, Cork, Tipperary and Limerick being sold off or given away for similar reasons. In the early years of the twentieth century, Edith Somerville and her writing partner and cousin, Violet Martin, visited north Kerry. She later wrote about 'the thrill' that 'shook' both of them when they cast eyes on Kerry Beagles 'among their native mountains' for the first time. She was enchanted by the 'tall, romantic creatures' she saw there, with their 'long, pendant, unrounded ears and lovely eyes'. The packs of Kerry Beagles that were kept on family estates may have diminished, but Somerville wrote that there were still many farmers who kept 'a hound or two to hunt with the Sunday pack'.

In 1907, Rawdon Lee had believed that there was only one united pack of Kerry Beagles still in existence, when 'not many years ago' they had been 'the most popular hounds in the south of Ireland'. He feared that there was a real possibility of this 'fine old variety' of scent hound becoming 'as extinct as the Dodo'. Indeed, he thought that there was even a danger of them 'being forgotten altogether'. Lee's worst fears have not been realised, but the numbers of

Kerry Beagles and of all other hunting dogs kept in Ireland continued to fall through much of the twentieth century.

There were several reasons for that decline. World War One had a devastating impact on all hunting breeds, and also on their owners. Lieutenant Henry Wallis was the only son of Aubrey Wallis of Drishane Castle in County Cork, and a neighbour of Edith Somerville. This young man was killed in action at Ypres in the opening months of the war. A newspaper obituary remarked upon the 'extraordinary affection and spirit of camaraderie' that had existed between father and son, and the 'heavy blow' that had been dealt to the older man. According to the obituary, it had been 'the dream of the father' that his heir would one day 'take over the family pack of Kerry Beagles'. But it was not to be, and the pack was subsequently dispersed.

The economic slump that followed World War One, along with the break-up of many of the remaining old estates by the Irish Land Commission, resulted in most of the packs that had been privately owned by families like the Wallises being given to local hunt committees. These developed into the county packs that exist today throughout Ireland. However, one pack managed to survive that process, and now represents the only united pack of Kerry Beagles in the country.

Although hunting was primarily associated with the Irish gentry, it was not solely confined to that class. Instead, as Edith Somerville observed, there was a popular following among more substantial Irish farmers for 'trencher-fed' packs of Kerry Beagles, where the dogs were owned by a number of different individuals, and only came together as a pack for a specific hunt. However, the last surviving pack that lives in one kennel is the same one that Lee mentioned in 1907, and which may still be found in Knocklong in County Limerick. The Scarteen pack had been unmolested during the protests of the 1880s—perhaps because the local landlords were not regarded as harsh. The famous Scarteen hounds were also known as 'the Black and Tans', and it was from them that the counter-insurgency force raised by the British during the Irish War of Independence, who initially wore a mixture of khaki and rifle green uniforms, acquired their nickname.

The Scarteen pack is entirely made up of purebred Kerry Beagles. The Ryan family can claim to have kept a pack of these dogs for several centuries, and Chris Ryan is the latest family member to be Master of the Scarteen Hunt. It has been suggested that the Ryans, as Catholic gentry with Jacobite antecedents, had remained loyal to this breed for patriotic reasons. In the past 300 years there have been only eight Masters, and seven of them have been Ryans. One of them is said to have asked that the window of his bedroom be opened as he lay dying, and his hounds sent out to hunt, so that he might hear the music of their baying one last time. The fame of this hunt has spread, and visitors come from all over the world to follow the pack of Scarteen dogs. The hunt can include New York brokers, lawyers from Australia and businessmen from Germany.

Some of the dogs have been exported, to the United States, Australia and New Zealand, where they have fitted in well with the local hounds. Indeed, Irish dogs are contributing to the current revival of fox-hunting in Tasmania. As a local newspaper has recently reported, the 'sound of thundering hooves and baying hounds' now ring out for several months of every year near the small Tasmanian town of Bracknell. Unlike the Scarteen hunt, however, the dogs track an aniseed trail that is laid down by drag riders who go ahead of the main field. The pack is a relatively small one with just fourteen hounds, and is composed of three breeds: American and English Foxhounds, as well as a few Kerry Beagles.

The Kerry dogs are said by some to be a difficult breed to train, and were once dismissed in *The Field* as 'unruly' when judged by 'English Foxhound standards'. However, Chris Ryan has claimed that the Kerry Beagles have more 'fox sense' than any of their counterparts on the other side of the Irish Sea. Over the years the Ryans have been careful to avoid allowing one bloodline to dominate the pack, and there are usually six or seven lines running through the dogs. In honour of their pack, the members of the hunt wear black coats with tan collars.

There are many ways in which the Kerry Beagles differ from all the rest of Ireland's native breeds, and that is not just a question of their lack of recognition from kennel clubs outside Ireland. The Kerry Beagle was developed over the centuries to be a highly efficient hunting animal. We no longer expect Wolfhounds to chase wolves, or send Glen of Imaal terriers into badger setts. But Kerry Beagles are still primarily working in the role for which they were originally bred, at which they excel, and which they clearly relish.

It is still unusual to see them in the show ring, and, perhaps as a result, they have not been caught up in some of the controversies or fashions that have affected other breeds. However, in May of 2016, a Kerry Beagle bitch made history when she was placed in the winning group at a championship show for the first time. One of the dog's owners subsequently wrote a letter to *Dog World* in which he claimed that the breed was not receiving sufficient support from the Irish Kennel Club. He compared the Kerry Beagle with the Red and White Setter, suggesting that the kennel club had taken up the setter's cause only when efforts to conserve that breed were already well under way. I met Michael O'Dwyer at an all-breed show where he had entered two of his dogs. He had obtained both of them from Scarteen. Although they were both black and tan, he pointed out to me that this was not the only colouring for an authentic Kerry Beagle.

He has questioned the value of drag-hunting in maintaining the Kerry Beagle, claiming that it was compromising the purebred bloodlines of the dog by introducing new blood from England. Drag-hunting usually involves laying a scent of animal urine or droppings to which paraffin is sometimes introduced as a fixative so that the scent won't evaporate. Other sources can also be added to increase the strength of the scent. The sport has a long history in Ireland, and until recently the Kerry Beagle was the principal dog used, but as drag hunts have gained in popularity, other breeds have begun to be used more frequently.

These include the Trail Hound, a breed that originates in England's Fell country, and which has been bred out of the English Foxhound. It is said that the dog has been cross-bred in the past with Greyhounds. If true, that may explain why selective breeding has significantly improved the speed of the Trail Hounds. In fact, foxhounds are no longer accepted as participants in some English hunts due to their relative lack of pace. Trail Hounds are also considerably faster than the Kerry dogs, so there is an obvious temptation to cross-breed. However, it is reckoned to take roughly three generations of crossing before a dog will regain the speed of the current Trail Hound, which acts as a form of deterrent.

It now seems that two separate forms of drag-hunting have evolved. One of these involves the form of live hunting which is still dominated by the Kerry Beagle. The other involves trail-hunting, which is now dominated by the English dog. The first of these forms of hunting has attracted followers in Ireland from a wide range of social backgrounds, and its participants seem to share a high level of commitment to the maintenance of the Kerry Beagle. The growth and popularity of these drag hunts may offer a more secure future to a breed that has been threatened with extinction for over 100 years—provided, that is, cross-breeding does not take place on an extensive scale. However, once again, that still seems preferable to allowing the dogs to be bred from too small a gene pool.

Kerry Beagles are the rarest of all of Ireland's native dogs, and also the most difficult to obtain. Although they are highly affectionate and intelligent, and relate well to children, they may not be ideally suited to every family since they require a lot of exercise, with lengthy walks and free runs every day. The current numbers of Kerry Beagles may be low, but they seem steady. The demise of this breed has been predicted many times, but it has always managed to survive, and if there is one outstanding quality that this dog had displayed over the centuries, it is its staying power. It holds that in common with the oldest of Ireland's native terriers: the Soft-Coated Wheaten.

'War of the Scissors': the Irish Soft-Coated Wheaten Terrier

There are four native breeds of terrier in Ireland, and at least two of these, the Kerry Blue and the Irish, are generally believed to be descended from the Wheaten Terrier. In the 'First Great Show of all kinds of Terriers' staged by Charles Cruft in 1886, there were references in *The Illustrated London News* to the presence of 'wheaten-coloured Irish specimens'. Nonetheless, the Wheaten was the last of the Irish terriers to have its own breed club. It was also the last to be recognised as a show dog. In fact, the Wheaten did not even acquire its official name until 1937, and it was not until 1973 that the Irish Soft-Coated Wheaten Terrier, to give the dog its full title, was accepted in its own breed class by the American Kennel Club.

Since then, there have been a number of disputes and controversies over which of the current strains of the Wheaten breed has the best claim to represent the original terrier. Despite all of that, the Wheaten has proved to be the most popular of Ireland's native terriers, and unlike its Irish relatives its future existence is not considered to be at risk.

If the tide of popular appeal has turned against some of the other native Irish breeds, it has decidedly run in favour of this one.

Like most of the other Irish breeds, there have been claims that the Wheaten Terrier is of ancient origin. 'Like the hallowed Saint Patrick himself,' one admirer wrote, 'it is believed the breed dates back as far as the hills and bogs of Ireland.' That writer does concede that the proof of such an imaginative assertion is 'buried in antiquity', and there is little written documentation of the Wheaten until the mid nineteenth century. The same writer suggests it was from the 'silver tongues' of Ireland's folk singers, wandering scholars, storytellers and poets that the authentic stories of these ancient dogs were passed 'from one generation to the next'.

In fairness, there is no doubt that terriers similar in size to the Wheaten were used for many generations in Ireland to hunt foxes and badgers, to keep houses and farms free of vermin, and to provide Irish homes with a regular supply of small game. Many of those dogs would probably not have been considered as pets in the modern sense. They were working animals, and it is most unlikely that they were mollycoddled by their owners, who were often hard pressed to feed themselves. However, according to Dr E. S. Montgomery, a historian of Irish terriers, these dogs were also valued for their courage and sporting 'gameness', and for their ability to hunt otters in canals and rivers, and to draw badgers from their setts.

Others took a less benign view of Ireland's terriers. An article published in the London *Times* in 1864, for example, sought to identify the differences between respectable English dogs and disreputable 'Irish curs'.

This anonymous English gentleman believed that 'the number of worthless dogs in Ireland [was] prodigious'. He accused the Irish dogs of annoying passengers and frightening horses 'by their furious barking on public roads'. He claimed they went 'prowling over the country at night', attacking flocks of sheep and killing them. Most of these animals, he suspected, were also kept 'for poaching purposes', and he was greatly offended that their owners often chose to hunt illegally 'during the hours of worship on Sunday'. The article concluded:

> In England—a comparatively honest and justice-loving land—the canine race bark at a thief: but in the sister isle they give warning at the approach of the police!

According to one Canadian writer, the Irish peasantry needed a small dog that 'would not draw the attention of the English', and the Wheaten Terrier was ideal because he 'appeared to be of very little value' and 'rarely got a second look'. However, this interpretation of Ireland's canine history seems to ignore the presence of small terrier breeds in other countries, including England, which were not oppressed by any colonial power. The same writer conjures up a scene of domestic intimacy between Irish peasants and their dogs, whom he imagined were treated as part of the family, and apparently shared the same 'daily meals of potatoes and buttermilk'. However, this writer also claims that any dogs who turned out to be poor hunters would soon end up 'in the stew pot'—which may seem incompatible with treating them as cherished family members.

At the end of the nineteenth century, one Dublin owner of a Wheaten Terrier insisted that his family had kept 'a special strain of Irish terriers' for many generations. He said that these Irish terriers were 'wheaten coloured' and 'open-coated', meaning their coats were soft and without an undercoat, which sounds very like the modern Wheaten Terrier. The same owner also claimed that these dogs would fight 'until nearly killed, if once provoked'. However, it is not certain if the animals that he described were Wheaten Terriers, or another related breed, since at that time 'Irish Terriers' was often used as a collective term to cover all the various types of terrier to be found in Ireland.

In general, the differences between the various breeds of Irish terrier were not well-defined until the 1880s, since there was no need to do so, and there had also been considerable interbreeding between the different types. As a consequence, it was not unusual for a litter of pups to contain several different colours, and this tendency was only brought under control in the course of the last century through the introduction of selective breeding. The precise definition of the Wheaten Terrier breed was further complicated by the fact that its dominant colour is not confined to an Irish breed. Dogs from other countries, such as the Cairn Terrier, can also be wheaten, and perhaps that illustrates the drawbacks of determining any breed of dog solely by the colour or texture of its coat.

It was not until the 1930s that a group of enthusiasts tried to obtain recognition by the Irish Kennel Club for the Wheaten Terrier as a distinct breed. At a field trial of terriers in 1932, a Wheaten Terrier had caught the eye of some of those present, among them Dr Gerard Pierse, a breeder of Kerry Blues. At that time the Wheaten Terrier seemed to be heading towards extinction, and the more stylised Kerry Blues and Irish Terriers had overtaken the older breed in popularity. Dr Pierce was one of those who could see the future potential of the Wheaten, as well as the danger of extinction that it faced, and so could his friend Patrick Blake. Both men were experienced dog-breeders, and were also well placed to advance the cause of the Wheaten dog.

Patrick Blake had grown up hunting rabbits with terriers in the Tipperary countryside. When he moved to Dublin, his affection for the terrier breeds remained intact, and he kept and showed Irish Blue Terriers (as he preferred to call the Kerry dog). When the Working Terrier Association was set up in 1929, Blake became its first secretary—an office he would hold for the next twenty-two years. In the 1930s he also served as a member of the Irish Kennel Club Council. Dr Pierse came from Tralee in County Kerry, and, like Blake, he had retained his interest and involvement in terrier breeding after he moved to Dublin. In the early 1930s, Pierse was secretary of the All-Ireland Kerry Blue Terrier Club, and was widely accepted as the 'first amongst Irish breeders and authorities' when it came to terriers.

In 1934, Pierse and Blake founded a Wheaten Terrier Club, and its first priority was to fix the type by only using purebred Wheatens in future breeding programmes. The two men also began a campaign to have the dog recognised as a separate breed. In spite of the high regard in which they were held in breeding circles, this proved to be a challenging task.

There had been a lot of cross-breeding of Wheatens in previous generations, and many doubted that the dog still existed in a purebred form. For some, all that Wheaten dogs seemed to hold in common was their colour, and their soft silky coat.

According to Dr Montgomery, an accepted authority on Irish breeds, the owners of Irish Terriers and Kerry Blue Terriers were 'the ones raising the loudest objections' to recognition of the Wheaten. Montgomery believed that these 'terrier men' felt the dog was too closely related to their own breeds to be truly distinct. Several applications for recognition by the Irish Kennel Club had been turned down, ostensibly because of the name that had been suggested. The original proposal was to call the dog the 'Irish Wheaten Terrier', but this was criticised by the owners of Irish and Glen of Imaal terriers since the standard points of both those breeds already included wheaten as an acceptable colour. Eventually, after much internal debate and wrangling, it was agreed that if the name of the breed were to be the 'Irish Soft-Coated Wheaten Terrier', then the Irish Kennel Club would grant full recognition.

On St Patrick's Day in 1937, Wheatens were invited to parade at the annual dog show to mark and celebrate this recognition. On the same day the following year, ten dogs took part in the first Wheaton breed class. A dog called Kingdom Leader, owned by Patrick Blake, became the first champion, while the runner-up, Charlie Tim, was owned by Dr Pierse. The chairman of the Irish Kennel Club, Henry Fottrell, noted that the Wheatens 'attracted interest as representatives of an old Irish breed'. However, he thought that the ten show dogs were 'not very impressive', and expressed an opinion that 'time will be needed for an improvement in quality and numbers'. In the interim, a registry for the breed was opened, and if pedigree records were not available, a group was appointed by the Kennel Club to examine the dogs and decide whether each of them fitted the breed standard. A small number of dogs were then registered.

Numbers slowly increased over the next few years, but the growth in the breed's popularity that Fottrell had anticipated was delayed for obvious reasons by the outbreak of World War Two. Nonetheless, in 1943 Dr Pierse managed to convince the British Kennel Club to open a breed register, and by 1955 the Soft-Coated Wheaten Club of Great Britain was established. It took a further twenty years before the breed was allowed to compete for challenge certificates at Crufts.

There are some obvious similarities between the Wheaten and two other long-legged dogs: the Irish Terrier, and in particular the Kerry Blue. The adult dogs and bitches of all three breeds are roughly the same height and weight. They share more or less equal life expectancies. They all have minimal shedding of their coats, and all respond to training. They are all adaptable and active, and usually relate well to children. Of course, there are also differences between the three. These include distinctions of character and frame, but the most obvious are their respective colours. Not surprisingly, all Wheatens are required to be wheaten-coloured. Their pups are often darker, especially around the muzzle and ears, and this can continue into adolescence. However, all adult dogs must be uniformly wheaten if they are to compete in major exhibitions.

All three of these terriers require a relatively high degree of maintenance. However, the Wheaten might be considered the most demanding in this regard, and the reason is another of the breed's distinctive features: its fair coat. Many terriers have double coats to protect them from harsh weather conditions, but only the Wheaten has a wavy single coat that covers its entire body and head, and can appear to flow as the dog moves. Unlike many other terriers, the texture of the coat is, as its name indicates, soft to the touch and not wiry. Ironically, this signature coat has led to recurrent tensions between Wheaten breeders.

In the decade after it was recognised by the Irish Kennel Club, the popularity of the Wheaten grew in Ireland. Some of those showing Wheatens in competition came to believe that it was desirable to 'top and tidy' their appearance. The heads and necks of Wheatens began to be trimmed to make them from look neater and less shaggy. The legs and bodies of the dogs were also cut and styled to show off their clean terrier lines. This was not a radical reshaping of the terrier's appearance: in fact, it now appears quite modest and restrained.

The new approach to the show appearance was led by a passionate and committed breeder called Maureen Holmes, who has been described as the 'moving force' in the story of the Wheaten dog over six successive decades. The development of any breed often seems to depend upon the unwavering dedication of one individual, and Maureen Holmes seems to have been a striking example of this tendency. She also has an unusual flair for coining a colourful phrase: according to one account, she was determined not to have her dogs looking like 'walking piles of hay'. However, the founding fathers of the breed, Patrick Blake and Gerard Pierse, came from a background in which dogs were primarily judged by their performance in the field, and they were suspicious of any attempt to enhance the breed's appearance by styling its coat. Their steadfast opposition to Maureen Holmes's approach gave rise to what has been termed the 'War of the Scissors'.

This conflict was won decisively by Holmes, with the eventual inclusion of a trimming clause in the breed's standard points. Although Wheatens that have not been styled are still permitted to enter competitions, they are seldom seen in the show ring nowadays. Ironically, this dispute turned out to be less of a war than a skirmish in comparison to what was yet to come. And Maureen Holmes was to play a very different role in the next controversy that arose concerning the appearance of Wheatens.

One of the first challenges facing those who want to establish a new pedigree breed is to prove that the dog has been bred true, and the standard features have been fixed. There is sometimes a second problem, which can prove more intractable in the long run: how to ensure that the breed stays fixed, and that dogs in different countries do not begin to go down diverging paths of development. If they do, there is the risk that such separate development will eventually lead to two distinct breeds. That is, after all, what happened to the two breeds of Irish Setter. This problem is often most acute when the divergent strain develops in the United States, the country that holds the largest number and proportion of pedigree dogs in the world, but that is just what happened to the Irish Wheaten.

Our American Cousins

In 1947, the first Wheatens had arrived in North America, but these dogs were not able to gain a sustainable foothold. However, in the late 1950s a number of new terriers arrived from Ireland. From this point, the Wheatens began to be bred with a serious purpose in the United States, and they started slowly to gain in popularity. In 1965 a Wheaten stud book was formed, and eight years later the breed was officially recognised by the American Kennel Club. Until then, Wheatens were only exhibited in the miscellaneous class in dog shows; from October of 1973, they could be shown in regular classes. By then, there were around 1,100 Wheatens registered in the United States, and the dog was already beginning to look rather different from the terriers that had arrived from Ireland fifteen or so years previously.

According to one critic, this had occurred because 'more flashy and plush dogs were encouraged by the fad of the show ring'. Something similar also took place in the UK, and by the end of the 1970s, three different strains of Wheaten had emerged. There was still the original Irish type, which could clearly be identified as a form of terrier. But now there was also an English type, which was rather larger, heavier, and in some critics' eyes, 'fluffier', as well as an American dog whose coat was woollier, and whose shape seemed more angular.

Given the size and commercial value of the American pedigree dog market, there is always a tendency for US standards to affect the development of breeds that originated in Europe. Not long after its arrival in the United States, it appeared that the Wheaten was moving away from its original Irish standard, and beginning to develop a heavier and woollier coat. What is more, it also seemed that heavier coats were popular with the American public. In that context, it may not seem surprising that American, and to a lesser extent English, breeders concentrated on developing their own strains, and that fewer of them were inclined to produce dogs based on the original Irish standard. It was also predictable that Irish breeders would object to the dog diverging in type from that of the country in which it had originated.

The differences were most noticeable in the early years of a Wheaten's life. While the Irish pups were clearly terriers, litters produced by heavy-coated American dogs were less so—indeed, they were often described as resembling teddy bears. The heavier-coat type also matured sooner than those with a light coat. This was preferred by breeders since it meant their dogs could compete in shows at an earlier age. The coat of the Wheaten is one of its defining features. It has been described as the 'crowning glory' of the breed, and its central importance is evident even in the dog's name. However, concerns were soon expressed that breeding primarily for the coat would come to affect other aspects of the dog's appearance and character. What made this issue more acute was the fact that there was no obvious meeting point between the light and the heavy-coated dogs.

That was because it was not deemed desirable, or even possible, to breed a dog whose coat was in between the two principal types. An American Wheaten that is mated with another can only produce a heavy-coated dog. However, a purebred Irish Wheaten that is mated with an American type will only give birth to a light-coated pup, because the Irish gene is always dominant. If the Wheatens are of mixed heritage, then some of their pups will tend to be light-coated, and some will conform to the American type. In some cases of mixed heritage the Irish genes may still be dominant, but the dogs do acquire a somewhat heavier coat, and those Wheatens can now be further subdivided into 'Traditional Irish' and 'Heavy Irish' dogs.

By the 1970s, Maureen Holmes had grown deeply concerned about what was happening to Wheatens in other countries. After a trip to America she felt that Americans were breeding for the coat at the expense of the true terrier type. 'We do not want to make balloons of fluff,' she wrote. 'We want terriers in type and character.' She later referred to the American Wheatens as 'soft white nothings'. In another article she claimed that visiting Irish judges could not even recognise their own Wheaten breed in American shows.

Maureen Holmes had devoted most of her adult life to the preservation and promotion of the Irish Wheaten Terrier, and she was convinced that Americans were now ruining her beloved dog and her life's work. She held an equally low opinion of English breeders. In fact, she believed that the purebred Wheaten had first been mutated in Great Britain. She also suspected that other breeds of dogs had been secretly crossed with the Irish terrier in Britain and America, and believed that explained the changes she could observe in the dog's health and appearance.

Most of all, Maureen Holmes was concerned that the breeding programmes followed in the UK and United

States had forfeited the unique terrier temperament of the Wheaten. As a result, she concluded that American and British breeders had created what was, in effect, a new sub-species of the original Irish dog. It would seem that some American breeders tacitly acknowledged some of her opinions. As one Irish critic has pointed out, the American standard description of the breed removed the terms 'spirited', 'game' and 'intelligent' from its original phrasing, and replaced those three words with just one: 'happy'.

Shortly before her death, Maureen Holmes wrote a speech that she intended to deliver to the Eighth World Congress of Kennel Clubs, which was being held in Trinity College, Dublin, over a July weekend in 1995. The theme of her address was 'Ireland's Native Breeds', but, as she was in hospital, she was unable to deliver the speech in person. Instead it was read for her, and although she was not present, the speech showed that neither the passage of time nor serious illness had dimmed her passion for the Wheaten dog.

She began by describing her own involvement with the breed, which had started some sixty-three years previously. She said that she had watched with pride as the popularity of the Wheaten had spread 'from one country to another'. However, she added that she had also watched in dismay as American dogs of 'a different type, style and build' had 'almost decimated' the original Irish terrier and brought the breed 'to the brink of disaster'. She believed that nature had 'designed this Irish dog as one of late maturity', but it seemed to her that the Americans were not prepared to wait for this maturity, and somehow 'an alien wooly coat ' had been 'engineered into the breed'.

Holmes reckoned that the original standard points had been drawn up by 'people who have forgotten more about dogs than many others will ever know'. She insisted that 'only owners in the country of origin have a complete knowledge of that country's dogs', and therefore only those in the country of origin were 'entitled to make any changes in the standard'. She claimed that, as well as the Official Irish Standard, there were now three others: the English, the American and the Canadian. She dismissed the last three as being drawn up by people for whom dog-breeding was not a vocation, but merely 'a lucrative hobby'.

She ended her address by claiming that 'the nine Irish native breeds are part of our cultural heritage'. She believed that dog-breeders like herself were:

> only the custodians of these breeds, [with] a moral obligation to cherish and protect them to the best of our ability so that they may be handed on to our successors in the shape and form originally laid down for them.

While the integrity of Maureen Holmes's views may not be impugned, some of her underlying assumptions are, at least, open to question.

It is simply not true to suggest that the Wheaten dog had remained unchanged through untold Irish generations. There are few mentions of Irish terriers before the nineteenth century, and when these do occur, they usually suggest a type of dog rather than a distinct breed. The ultimate roots of the Wheaten may lie in ancient Ireland, but its early owners paid little if any attention to a precise breed standard. Images of Wheaten Terriers that date from the late nineteenth century do not reveal a consistent appearance, and the reason they are variable is because the Wheaten Terrier was still in the process of being bred into uniformity. It is also unrealistic to assume that the standards set for a dog that was originally intended to be a working animal on a farm should continue to be followed when that role has ended and the dog has become a family pet in an urban environment.

The changes that Maureen Holmes lamented were also signs of the adaptability and popularity of the Wheaten in societies outside Ireland. Since her speech was delivered to the Eighth Congress of Kennel Clubs, that popularity has been maintained. However, there have been other significant developments in more recent times. For a number of years, the American and British coats continued to grow heavier, but that generated new problems for their owners in terms of grooming and presentation. When new forms of illness and disease, such as renal dysplasia, were diagnosed as a breed problem, it may also have encouraged breeders in Britain and North America to revert to purebred Irish stock, or at least to mix the divergent strains of the breed.

Maureen Holmes died in 1996, but I think she would be gratified to learn that in recent years there has been renewed interest outside Ireland in the Irish type. Growing numbers of Irish Wheatens are reported to have featured in show contests, and more also seem to have been used in breeding programmes. Of course, there are still Wheatens in the United States who have woolly, rather than silky, coats. However, they aren't permitted to compete in show classes as Irish Soft-Coated Wheaten Terriers since they don't meet the breed standard. In fact, the 'American Wheaten Terrier' does not exist as a recognised breed, and the term is often used as a pejorative expression for Wheatens with woolly coats.

Even so, it should be stressed that this distinction is purely external, and there is no discernable difference between the two types of Wheaten in temperament or character.

Ms Holmes would doubtless be reassured to know that the 'American coat', which she despised and feared, is still not recognised as the breed standard, and that the Irish coat remains the only one officially recognised as 'Wheaten' by the Irish Kennel Club and the Fédération Cynologique Internationale. She might be pleased to learn that Wheatens have retained much of their 'natural' look, and are still not highly stylised when they enter the show ring. I presume that she would also be delighted that there are now reckoned to be more Wheatens in the world than any other native Irish terrier breed.

Maureen Holmes might be less happy with other developments that have affected the dog-breeding business. I can imagine she would be horrified to discover that the first attempts at producing a new wave of 'designer dogs' were already well under way at the time the Eighth World Congress of Kennel Clubs took place in Dublin. The notion that breeders would deliberately mate two recognised pedigree dogs simply in order to produce a cross-breed seems likely to have mystified and appalled her. She might also be taken aback to see the resemblance between her own beloved breed and the strain of Labradoodle dog that sports a curled and wheaten-coloured coat. But, as I think the history of the Wheaten demonstrates, dogs can be affected by changes in fashion almost as much as human beings. Nowadays, the Wheaten Terrier is the most popular of all Irish native breeds in the United States, but there was a time when it was challenged for that position by what many would consider the most glamorous of all Irish dogs.

'The Only Dog for Ireland':
the Irish Red Setter

When I was about seven years of age, I was roused in the middle of the night by my mother. I followed her downstairs, rubbing the sleep from my eyes. She had wanted to introduce me to a new addition to our extended family. The latest arrival was a young Red Setter bitch called Sheelagh, whom one of my uncles had just acquired. Sheelagh was around ten months old, and stood stock still in the middle of our living room. She seemed very shy and reserved, and trembled as I came nearer to stroke her rich red coat. Her eyes were dark brown, almond shaped, and seemed wonderfully expressive. Her legs were feathered, and her tail was plumed. There was also a small blaze of white on her chest. I felt in awe of her physical beauty, and determined in that moment that one day I would have a Red Setter of my own.

At that time, my uncle and aunt lived near the small village of Glasdrumman in the heart of the mountains of Mourne that are said to sweep down to the sea. My uncle's experiences in war may have hardened him, but he was not a sentimental man, and he had not bought Sheelagh as a pet, but to be a working gun dog. I often stayed with him and my aunt in Glasdrumman, and on some occasions he allowed me to accompany him and his friends when they went to shoot on Slieve Binnion, or Spence's Mountain. I watched as the red dogs were slipped from their leashes to range through the heather, their noses held high in the air, eager to catch any scent of a grouse or pheasant.

Suddenly, one or two of the dogs would stop in their tracks and stand motionless. Their noses would point to one horizon; their tails were held straight in the opposite direction. One of their front paws would be raised and cocked. The instinct of many domestic dogs when they spot a bird is to chase it. Generations of selective breeding, along with hours of patient training, had conditioned these setters to control that first impulse. Instead, they quivered with excitement as they waited for the game to rise into the sky. There was an intensity of focus that seemed to tighten their whole bodies, which always thrilled me.

Sheelagh was a gentle soul. I remember one day a neighbouring farmer called to inform us that the little bitch had been stealing his eggs. I searched outside our cottage until I found a stash of the eggs she had taken. Sheelagh had managed to carry each one for a mile or so without breaking any of them. I had no idea why she had taken the eggs, but I was amazed at how soft her mouth must have been, and how carefully she had carried them. Alas, my uncle was not so impressed. He thought that Sheelagh was too easily distracted, and lacked the discipline of a first-rate field dog. Eventually, I was told that she had been passed on to one of his friends, where she would find a new identity as a family pet. It was much later that I discovered my uncle had not taken Sheelagh to a new home, but to the vet where she was put to sleep. There are mountainy sheep in the Mournes and Sheelagh had been seen worrying some ewes – a capital offense, in my uncle's eyes.

There are four principal types of pedigree setter: the English, the Gordon, the Irish Red and White and the Irish Red. The two Irish breeds are believed to be the oldest of that group, and the Red Setter is the most popular, and now the most numerous. For me, Reds are the catwalk models of their tribe: glamorous and effortlessly elegant, but with a touch of devilment, some might say madness, in their genetic mix. It is no surprise to me that their owners have included Russian tsars, US presidents and Hollywood movie stars. It also seems appropriate that the dog favoured by Charles Stewart Parnell, the charismatic leader adored by James Joyce, should be one of this breed. Indeed, Parnell insisted that his faithful setter stay with him while he lay on his deathbed, abandoned by most of his former followers. The Red's country of origin is, of course, Ireland, and both the all-red and the Red and White Setters are likely to have been bred out of some mixture of land spaniels. There was a need for a hunting dog of stamina and speed who would prove adaptable to the rough Irish terrain, with its bogs and marshes, and that required a larger frame than most land spaniels possessed. At the same time, the Irish Setter needed a lightness of build that could carry him over uneven and boggy land.

By the late sixteenth century, John Keys, otherwise known as Johannes Caius, the pioneering naturalist who was particularly interested in canine anatomy, described the 'setter dogge'. He thought that the setter's name was 'consonant and agreeable to his quality'. However, the dog described by Dr Caius seems to bear little relation to current Irish Setters. There are also references from the same period to a dog described in Irish as the *madra ruadh* ('red dog'), but it also seems unlikely that this relates directly to the animal we now know as the Irish Red Setter. It was not until the nineteenth century that the a solid red type emerged; until then, Irish Setters came in a variety of colours, and they were all regarded as belonging to the same breed.

By the start of the nineteenth century, setters had been bred systematically in Ireland for several centuries, usually by the local gentry, some of whom had already started to keep detailed stud records. Their goal was to produce a dog of superior hunting quality, and its colour was usually considered of secondary importance. Some families, such as the Rossmores of Monaghan, favoured the red and white colouring. Others, such as the Earls of Enniskillen, bred setters that were all-red, and culled any pups who carried white markings. However, most owners seemed relatively indifferent to colour, and it also seems likely that some English and Gordon Setters featured in the mix, for some dogs were born with black and tan colours, or with black tips on their flanks and legs. As the nineteenth century progressed, the colour of Irish Setters became almost as important as their noses and tracking abilities, and it grew more fashionable for members of the Irish aristocracy and gentry to own dogs that were solid red.

The growing popularity of all-red setters was related to the emergence of pedigree dog shows. Initially, as we have seen, many of these took place as a mere adjunct to traditional poultry shows or cattle auctions. In the early years, only gun dogs took part, and, not surprisingly, the prizes for their owners were often guns. At first, show dogs were supposed to be judged primarily by the character of the animal that had already been proved in the field. As I have mentioned, two of my relatives were involved in breeding and showing Red Setters at that time.

A separate class for setters had been established in Birmingham in the early 1860s, and Harry Blake Knox and his cousin William Hutchinson travelled frequently to England over the next few years to take part in shows there. They met with some success, and both owned champion setters. William's dog, Bob, became well known for his success in the ring. In 1864, Bob became the first Irish Setter to win the chief prizes at major shows in Birmingham, Cremorne and Islington. An editorial in *The Field* praised this 'blood-red Irish Setter' for his 'purity of colour', 'length and depth of frame' and 'fast look'. According to the editor, John Henry Walsh (who wrote under the (curious) pseudonym of 'Stonehenge'), Bob was the 'genuine article', and an 'enchanting dog' who was descended from 'the best blood in Ireland'. He noted that Bob possessed a 'very grand, sensible, expressive head' with a 'powerful loin', and limbs that were 'all bone and muscle'. He also paid tribute to his 'grace and endurance' and his 'capital feet and legs'. All in all, he regarded the dog as 'as good a sort as any known'.

This was not only a powerful endorsement of a single dog, but also of the entire breed, which Stonehenge praised for its 'gameness, courage, speed, endurance, intelligence, and talent'. His testimony appeared in a highly influential publication, whose readership was based on the upper echelons of English society, and on social classes who were devoted to traditional field sports. *The Field* was soon to become directly involved in the formation of the world's first kennel club, and the club's stud book, which soon became a bible for dog-breeders, was compiled for many years in the offices of that magazine. But, of course, *The Field* was never simply and solely about dogs, or even sporting events for that matter. From the start, it was also intimately connected with issues of social status. In that context, the strength of the imprimatur given by Stonehenge was likely to seem highly persuasive.

However, this editorial endorsement by *The Field* also drew out some critics of the setter; one of them thought Bob 'too heavy both in frame and head', as well as being 'obviously overtopped'. The same critic did concede that he had 'reason to believe' that William's dog was 'thoroughly good' in the field. The latter opinion was endorsed by Harry Blake Knox, who owned Bob's sibling, Dan. Harry believed that his setter was a better-looking specimen than Bob (and Dan would also win the Birmingham prize), but he also acknowledged that Bob had a better nose and greater powers of endurance. In Harry's opinion, Bob was, therefore, the better dog, and a more deserving champion. As it turned out, both dogs, but Bob in particular, would play a significant role as sires in the future of the breed. Indeed, Bob's son, Ranger, won at the Birmingham show a few years after his father. Bob sired many pups, and his descendants played a crucial role in establishing the breed, and not just in Ireland. In 1876, his grandson, a dog called Elcho, was exported to the United States, and became the first Irish Red Setter to win a championship event there. Elcho went on to sire 197 pups of his own, and is believed to be the ancestor of almost every Irish Red Setter now living in North America.

The 1860s was a seminal decade in the development of dog shows. The early exhibitions had proved to be enormously popular with the general public, and were a huge commercial success. Before very long, they had been opened to non-sporting breeds: a crucial development that gave birth, in effect, to the modern concept and industry of pedigree dog-breeding. The 1860s were also very turbulent years in Irish history. A secret revolutionary organisation had been founded in Dublin at the end of the previous decade. It called itself the Irish Republican Brotherhood, but its members became better known as the Fenians—named after the warrior caste of Celtic legend. Their goal was an insurrection against British rule in Ireland, and they hoped to create an Irish Republic by force of arms. By 1865 the Fenians had gathered large supplies of weapons and thousands of followers, but the British moved decisively against them, imprisoning their leaders and closing down their newspaper. In 1866, habeas corpus was suspended in Ireland, and hundreds more Fenians were arrested.

All of this turmoil seems to have had little impact, at least initially, on Harry Blake Knox. Admittedly, he was a landowner in the west of Ireland, where the Fenians had comparatively little influence and relatively few members. The principal concern of tenant farmers in the west was land reform, which the Fenian leadership did not support because they feared it might distract from a more important goal: the winning of Ireland's political freedom. In time, the campaign for land reform would come to preoccupy Harry Blake Knox's mind, but in the spring of 1866 what concerned him and his cousin was not the threat of a land war, or even a Fenian uprising, but a number of letters that had appeared in a recent edition of *The Field*.

This all began as a polite discussion of the 'black tip theory'. A breeder called John Walker disputed the claim that he said had been made by William Hutchinson and Harry Blake Knox at the recent Birmingham dog show.

According to Walker, they had maintained in public that 'any admixture of black colouring' in an Irish Setter could only 'emanate from an infusion of the Gordon [Setter] strain'. In Walker's account, they had claimed that this contaminated the dog's pure Irish blood, and 'ought to be ignored'. Walker disputed their view, and suggested that the 'purest and oldest strain of Irish Setter' had a 'slight tinge' of black on the tips of its ears and muzzle. He denied that this came from any 'black infusion' of Gordon Setter blood. In the next issue he was contradicted by William Hutchinson, who stated emphatically that the 'only true colour' of the Irish Setter was 'a very deep rich blood-red', which should be 'free from any mixture of black hair altogether'.

The correspondence went back and forth, slowly gaining in personal acrimony, until a letter appeared in the magazine that changed the nature of the debate. The anonymous writer clearly regarded the Gordon as a superior breed of setter, and derided the abilities of the Irish dog in the most scathing of terms. According to this writer, Irish Setters had 'neither pace, nose, courage, nor endurance'. He claimed to have known them for the previous fifty years, but had been more than happy to 'give them up' and write them off as a 'worthless' breed.

Harry Blake Knox was outraged by these calumnies, and *The Field* published his passionate and lengthy response in the next issue of the magazine. He began by insisting that the dogs that he and his cousin had exhibited in Birmingham should always be described as Irish *Red* Setters, and not simply as Irish, because 'every mongrel breed in Ireland is called an Irish Setter'. He then proceeded to deny the 'gross libels written by anonymous writers' that had been directed against the dog he had known and bred for many years. He was sure that those writers had 'never walked behind, much less shot over, a well-bred Irish Red Setter, if they found him wild, bad-nosed, sluggish, or unenduring'.

Harry then described at considerable length what he believed were the defining features of a genuine Irish Red Setter. Although much of the detail he gave may seem forensic in its detail, there is also evidence of a strong emotional attachment to his dogs. He describes the setter's eyes, for example, as a 'rich hazel or bright brown', but also mentions that they should be 'kind, sensible and loving'. He speaks with obvious affection of what he considers are the special features of his own favourite dog, which he judges to be superior and 'unlike any of his kind'. He also pays a warm tribute to that dog's mother, whom he says had often done 'a whole day's work, and pupped a healthy litter the day after'. For Harry Blake Knox, the Irish Red Setter is 'the fastest, most enduring, fine-nosed and most willing' of all sporting breeds. He concludes by claiming that it is truly 'the only dog for Ireland'.

Harry added a revealing postscript, in which he mentions that a black-and-tan setter bitch 'from England', which he had once somehow acquired, had been 'accidentally lined' by a red dog of his. Subsequently, she threw 'three red pups all showing black on their ears and backs'. Harry's final comment is terse and to the point: 'I, of course, drowned them.' In the twenty-first century, this casual admission may seem not only shocking, but incomprehensible. How could this man cull the healthy pups of a dog that he clearly loved? In the context of the time, there is another explanation for his actions, and one that would have occurred to any reader of *The Field*: he culled the pups *because* he loved the breed and wished to preserve its integrity. Our attitudes may have changed considerably in the decades that have passed since 1866, but it is worth remembering that the BBC documentary *Pedigree Dogs Exposed* was able to report instances of healthy pedigree pups still being culled in 2008, and I doubt if the practice has died out entirely to this day.

The correspondence about setters continued in the pages of *The Field* for several more months, with the balance of letters tending to favour Harry's views. His insistence that the breed should always and only be called the 'Irish Red Setter' had long-term effects, since that is how these red dogs came to be known. I have quoted at length from his defence of the Irish breed because, in some respects, I regard Harry Blake Knox as a representative figure of his time and social background. From an early age he combined a consuming interest in the natural world with a concomitant passion for hunting. Shooting birds helped him to study them up close, and Harry was eventually to bequeath a large collection of those he had shot, and whose eggs he had taken, to the Natural History Museum in Dublin. He was also an early disciple of Darwin, and liked to describe himself as a progressive 'Free Thinker', much to the distress of his daughters, whose religious views were more conventional.

That may also help to explain why he recommended the culling of setter pups whose black or white markings, in Harry's view, compromised the purity of their colour: Harry and his cousin William were committed to the idea of an all-red dog. But they also understood that the setter was a hunting dog, who found his true meaning and identity in the field. They would, in all likelihood, have been confused and confounded to see the ways in which the breed has subsequently developed.

Show and Field

The Irish Red Setter Club was founded in Dublin in 1882, which makes it one of the first breed clubs to be established in Ireland. The breed standard was drawn up and approved a few years later. This standard included a 100-point scale, with a given number of points awarded for each of the dog's physical attributes. It specified, for example, that the head of the dog should be twice the length of the width between its eyes; that the jaws should be of nearly equal length, with a perfect scissor bite; and that the colour should be a deep red chestnut shade. In many respects this was in line with the various points that Harry Blake Knox had outlined in his correspondence with *The Field* twenty years earlier, and I am sure he was delighted to learn that the new standard specified that there should be 'no trace whatever' of black markings. The points system was later dropped, but the standard has remained largely unchanged in most countries where the breed is now formally recognised by its national kennel club. In the latter half of the twentieth century the Irish Red Setter became popular in many different parts of the world. Indeed, it became the most popular of all Irish breeds. There were many possible reasons for that, including the intrinsic beauty of the dog as well as external factors.

In 1962, the Walt Disney Company released a movie called *Big Red*, which was based on a best-selling novel of the same name by Jim Kjelgaard. The book and film tell the story of a champion Red Setter. The film is somewhat similar in sentiment and theme to the better-known movies *Old Yeller* and *The Yearling*. Like them, its primary focus is less on the story of an animal than on the nature of the relationship between a young boy and his father—or, in the case of *Big Red*, his father figure. In the movie, Walter Pidgeon plays an obsessive dog owner who only considers his Irish Setter as a potential winner of dog shows, and not as his companion in life. A young boy comes to work for him, and develops a strong mutual bond with the setter. When the dog is scarred so badly in an accident that he can never be exhibited again, Pidgeon's character realises that his emotional connection with the setter, and by extension with the young boy, is of greater value than the first prize in any dog show.

The movie follows a fairly simple narrative, and it was one that proved very popular with American audiences. It may have contributed to the significant increase in the number of setters registered in the United States in the early 1960s, though this was not on the same scale as a dramatic surge in setter ownership that occurred in the following decade. The movie also touches upon some of the growing conflicts that had developed elsewhere in the dog-breeding industry. In particular, there is the implication that dog shows, and the pursuit of canine perfection they can entail, in some ways damage the closeness of human relationships with dogs.

When Harry Blake Knox and William Hutchinson first exhibited their Red Setters in shows of the 1860s, the breed still retained its undisputed status as a field dog with highly developed hunting instincts. Indeed, the vigorous defence of the Irish Red Setter that Harry and William advanced in the pages of *The Field* is wholly based on their positive assessment of the dog as a sporting breed. As Raymond O'Dywer has observed, in the early years a single 'fraternity' of owners and breeders attended both field and show events. At that stage, the two sports were 'indivisible', and the same gentlemen 'owned the dogs, shot over them, and field-trialed and showed them'. Since then, the breed has tended to become divided into show dogs and field setters, and at times relations between the owners and breeders of these two types have been strained.

From the 1860s, Irish Setters enjoyed a great deal of success in the show ring. However, until recently, the achievements of the all-red dogs in field trials were much less impressive. Between 1874 and 1948, the Irish Red Setter won 760 show championships. In the same period, the breed could muster only five field champions. It was hardly surprising that this led many breeders to favour the show over the field type. Indeed, by the 1940s it seemed as if the Irish Red Setter was paying a price for its triumphs in the ring, since the dog was fast disappearing from any sporting or field event. According to Jerry Thomas, a field enthusiast, 'the show-oriented majority established and controlled type', and the result of this was 'a sportsman's worst nightmare, the unbearable loss of respect among peers'. In that context, an outcross programme was considered necessary by some owners in the United States if the breed were to survive as a working dog. This was to lead to a significant division in the history of the Irish Red Setter breed.

Some field dog owners began to cross other gun dogs into their setter bloodlines. The pups were then bred back into the setter lines, and then crossed again, and back to setter lines, and so forth. It is believed that up to five different breeds were mated with Red Setters, including the English Setter, the English Pointer, the Hungarian Vizsla and the Brittany Spaniel. This was done in the United States with the knowledge and approval of the Field Dog Stud Book. It is the normal practice of that stud book to consider dogs to be purebred after they have bred back into five generations of the original pedigree stock. These field dogs are still formally described as Irish Setters, but are now usually referred to simply as Red Setters to distinguish them from the show specimens, who remain known as Irish Red Setters.

Usually, the American Kennel Club also gives more or less automatic registration rights to any dogs with five-generation purebred pedigrees—once the paperwork that proves this have been delivered, and the registration fees have been paid. In 1975, however, the Irish Red Setter Club of America petitioned the American Kennel Club to deny this registration to the cross-bred field setters, and the club granted this request. It has been claimed by some that this denial was the result of pressure applied by show dog owners who objected to the outcrossing programme because they thought it had damaged the integrity of the original breed. It has also been alleged that some of those who objected did so because their own dogs had been losing field trials to the outcrossed setters.

Nowadays, working kennels often include dogs whose bloodlines come from both the original and the outcrossed specimens, but the tension between the two has not gone away. A recent article by Jerry Thomas in *Gun Dog* magazine recounted an attitude that can be found among some of those who favour field to show dogs. According to this interpretation, Red Setters, 'a hard hunting and respected breed a century or more ago', have been turned, or 'show-bred', into 'tall, gangling, feathery shadows of their former selves', and have become 'vapid beauty queens with no nose, drive or intelligence'.

There are certainly differences between the two types of dog. Show setters have thicker, longer, glossier and darker coats than the field type. The show dogs are also somewhat larger, less stocky and less broad than the field setter. Show setters are bigger in the chest and have longer legs. Their necks are also longer, and so are their ears, which are not set as high as those of the field specimen. Field setters often carry a considerable amount of white markings on their chests and feet, and sometimes on their muzzles and legs. According to one breeder of the field type, they run faster, with more purpose, and have greater range and stronger pointing instincts. He concedes that field dogs are 'not so much beautiful to look at' as the show setters, but still believes 'they are beautiful to watch perform'. I must agree with that sentiment.

It should also be acknowledged that training dogs for the field requires a high level of expertise and commitment. Field trials are very demanding of the dogs taking part, requiring them, in the words of Raymond O'Dwyer, to use not only their intelligence, but 'all their senses', judging 'the ground and the wind' in order to win the race for game in each competition. The amount of field trials in Ireland has risen in recent years, and they have become very popular in the United States, where they are often conducted on horseback. In some respects, the current divergence between field and show setters corresponds to a broader one between the United States and Europe that surfaces in other breeds. The US market for pedigree dogs is by far the largest in the world, and there are obvious differences between American and European tastes in several areas. Given the dominance of the United States in so much of contemporary popular culture, there is, perhaps, an underlying suspicion that American breeders will in some sense commandeer European dogs and make them their own, just as European fairy tales have been transformed by Disney movies, and then exported back to the countries where those tales originated. This was clearly the fear of Maureen Holmes as far as the Wheaten Terrier was concerned.

There are, of course, owners of Red Setters who would not identify with either field or show camps. Their dogs may not have been outcrossed with any other breeds, but they would seldom take them into any show ring. Such dogs are sometimes described as 'Old Stock Irish Setters', and they may well be the closest to the type of Red Setter that was first exhibited in the middle of the nineteenth century. Perhaps they also indicate a possible future for the breed. There was a time, after all, when there was no conflict between show and field setters, and the current divergence of the two types may one day be resolved, and the breed united once again.

Some issues have proved somewhat easier to resolve. From the 1940s, the Irish Red Setter breed began to present multiple cases of dogs suffering from progressive retinal atrophy, better known as PRA. This eye disease comes in several forms, but both the all-red setter and the Red and

White Setter had become genetically disposed to its most acute type, which causes a progressive degeneration of the eye retina that will eventually lead to blindness. There is no known treatment for PRA, but fortunately DNA tests can now be used to identify carriers of the gene, and they can be eliminated from any breeding programme. As soon as this testing began to be implemented, the breed started to recover, and the incidence of PRA has dropped dramatically.

I achieved one of my ambitions as a child when I acquired an Irish Red Setter of my own. There was an advertisement for pups in a local newspaper that I happened to see. After I had nagged my mother relentlessly for several days, she agreed we could go and have a look at the litter. One evening soon afterwards, we were led by the pups' owner to his garage. On the way there, he told us that the dam had been stolen the week before, and he was keen to place her litter as soon as possible. He also advised us that a loose door had fallen a few days earlier and killed two of the pups. As a result, he believed that most of the litter were likely to prove gun-shy, and couldn't be worked in the field. The garage was dark and crowded with an assortment of motorcycles in varying states of repair, but I could make out a cluster of puppies huddled on a blanket in one corner. One long-legged pup made his way towards me, and when I knelt down, he licked my hand. 'Would you not like one of the smaller ones?' my mother asked nervously, but I had already made up my mind.

We decided to call him Rupert, and I was anxious to show the pup to my uncle, who had bred and kept Red Setters for much of his life. I wondered if he would reckon that I had made a good choice from the litter, and what tips he might give me about raising the pup. To my dismay, he looked at Rupert coldly, before informing me in equally cold and emphatic terms that I had made a serious mistake. 'You wanted a Red Setter because of his looks,' he told me, 'and that's the worst reason you could have. This is not a toy for you to play with, but a working dog. He deserves to be given the sort of life that you won't and can't offer him. The best thing you could do now is take him back to his former owner.'

As a child I was both shocked and disturbed by this reaction, and my stomach still turns when I think of it many years later. I had grown to respect my uncle's judgment as far as dogs were concerned, and I could not help but feel that there was a good deal of truth in what he had said. I was comforted by the thought that Rupert was gun-shy, and with the promise that I would do my best to fulfil all the obligations that an Irish Red Setter required. And I consoled myself by thinking that I could at least give him something that might sometimes have been missing in my uncle's treatment of his own dogs: genuine affection and delight in my dog's company.

Rupert was a red ball of energy when he was young, and his puppyhood seemed to last for many years. Like many of his breed, he was prone to becoming over-excited. He also had a strong sense of mischief, and he was very much a male dog, which seemed to mean that all the female members of my family adored him. In fact, they appeared to love him all the more because he was mischievous. Eventually, he made a graceful transition to a more dignified old age, but he never lost that spark of insatiable enthusiasm which I admired so much. In fact, his character continued to intrigue and fascinate me to the end of his long life.

In his last years, his eyesight was failing, his back had grown stiff, and he was completely deaf. There is something especially poignant in our knowledge that our dogs grow older faster than we do. It allows us to observe, in a compressed form, a journey through life from infancy through maturity to old age. And, as our dogs become infirm, we may also witness the stoicism and dignity with which they seem able to deal with their increasing physical limitations. It was hard to witness Rupert's decline, and we were beginning to face the possibility of letting him be euthanised—or 'destroyed', as Samuel Beckett might have said—but Rupert spared us that cruel necessity. My sister had taken him one evening for a walk in a park on the north side of Dublin, which she had chosen because traffic was expressly forbidden to pass through it. However, a motorcyclist ignored that ban. Rupert could not hear the sound of his bike's approaching wheels, nor my sister's desperate cries to warn him. The bike hit him at speed, shattering his hips, and he died almost at once.

As Raymond O'Dwyer, the president of the Irish Red Setter Club, observed some years ago, the fundamental nature of this breed was shaped by its original purpose and by its first environment. He suggested that the Irish Setter 'may have become a "salon dog" in some countries', but not in its native land, where its paws were still 'firmly planted in the soil', and that soil was 'black, energy-sapping peat'. This environment provided the context for dogs that had been shaped in their character and formed by the rigours of working on such a tough and exacting terrain.

Since my uncle hunted with his setters in the mountains around Glasdrumman, the breed has found a number of new occupations. They take part in obedience, tracking and agility competitions. They are also used as therapy dogs, and visit hospices, retirement homes and children's hospitals. All of these are worthwhile pursuits, but some underlying realities remain. If we scratch a show setter, we may still find a hunting dog just below the surface. And, as David Hancock has argued in his book *Gundogs*, there is a requirement, almost a moral obligation, to consider the setters' inherited instincts and their 'deeply implanted desire to use their noses'. I don't share my uncle's belief that Irish Red Setters can live a happy and fulfilled life only if they are worked in the field. But there is one lesson I learned from him that still makes sense to me: do not acquire any dog, pedigree, cross-breed or mongrel, unless you are well aware of its real needs and are prepared to meet them.

Old Dogs

The genetic status of a dog breed is determined by a number of different conditions. These include the location where the animal was bred; the number and type of dogs that helped to found its bloodline; and the speed and spread with which the breed developed. But the status of a dog to humans is also shaped by other factors.

All of the nine breeds that are considered to be native to Ireland occupy a place in the social history of our country. In that sense, they are also part of the story of the humans who share the island with them. Some of these dogs, like the Wolfhound, might appear to hold centre stage in Ireland's canine history; others, like the Glen of Imaal Terrier, can seem relegated to its margins. However, they can all be related to some of the turbulent events that have shaken Ireland over the course of several centuries. The histories of these breeds, like those of their owners, have been affected by wars, colonisation, famines, rebellions and other forms of communal conflict. At different times, these dogs have been both claimed and rejected by competing political, ethnic and social groups. As such, they present many of the contradictions that have seemed endemic in Ireland over the centuries.

Four of the nine native breeds have a historic association with the Irish gentry, although there are some fine distinctions of social class between each of these. Four of the other five breeds have a stronger connection with the Irish tenantry, but once again these can be further subdivided by several social, economic and geographic factors. The ancient Wolfhound differs in certain respects from both of these groups, perhaps because the name is attached to what are, essentially, two different breeds. The Wolfhound originated in Celtic Ireland, when its ownership was restricted to the old Gaelic nobility. The breed may not represent a democratic past, but it possesses a powerful resonance as a symbol of the country that existed before Ireland was conquered and colonised by the English. It seems fairly clear, however, that the modern Wolfhound has only a qualified claim to be considered as a true descendant of that ancient breed.

When the Irish Wolfhound was apparently resurrected towards the end of the nineteenth century, many of its patrons and most enthusiastic supporters were perceived as belonging to the landed gentry, and to the Protestant and Unionist community in Ireland—an impression that was reinforced when the Wolfhound was offered as a mascot to a regiment of the British Army. This was the context in which attempts were made by some radical Irish Nationalists to promote the Kerry Blue as an alternative national dog for the new and independent Irish state.

These attempts proved unsuccessful, and today the Kerry Blue is threatened with extinction, even in Ireland. I don't believe that will happen, but if it does, the Blue Terrier would not be the first breed of dog that has simply died out. In the course of the nineteenth and twentieth centuries, many other canine varieties disappeared: the Salish Wool Dog, the Blue Paul Terrier, the Chiribaya

Shepherd Dog and numerous other breeds. As Rosa Cima has observed, the extinction of any breed of dog has more similarities with the death of a language than with that of another species. When wild animals become extinct, it is usually because they have been hunted out of existence, or because their natural habitat has been destroyed. However, the natural habitat of domestic dogs has become our own homes. In that sense, their loss has a particular resonance and impact on human societies.

The extinction of dogs like the ancient Wolfhounds took place primarily because they had become functionally redundant: the role they had been designed to fulfil had ended, and so there was no longer any economic or practical purpose in breeding them. As Oliver Goldsmith noted over 200 years ago, it was 'as if nature meant to blot out the species, when they had no longer any services to perform'. When the modern Wolfhound was created almost a century later, it was for aesthetic and romantic reasons. However, the redundancy of certain breeds has not always been a bad thing, or one to be regretted. The humble Turnspit Dogs were no longer needed once machines were invented to perform their thankless and monotonous tasks. The fearsome Dogo Cubano was bred to chase and catch runaway slaves, and when slavery was abolished there was no longer any need to continue the breed, whose name had been tarnished by its barbaric occupation.

In the twentieth century, there were other reasons for the extinction of various dog breeds. The reasons are varied, and can seem mysterious, but in some cases the numbers of particular breeds fell so low that they became unsustainable;

in others, dogs have become so inbred that they began to develop serious genetic defects and were extinguished by disease. Sometimes, it even seems to have been a question of image. Either they failed to continue to interest the dog-owning public, or what they represented had become unfashionable.

No other animal has enjoyed the same extent of human affection and companionship as the domestic dog. It may have been praised as our best friend, yet no other creature has undergone such protracted human intervention and methodical control of its size, shape and character. Over the past 100 or so years, the rise of the commercial dog show has helped to move our attention away from the practical use of many breeds and towards their physical perfection. Dogs that once worked on farms, like the Kerry Blue Terrier, or hunted in the field, like the Red Setter, are now usually kept as family pets, or are bred for exhibition. It would be naïve to presume that dog shows are entirely responsible for this fundamental change: they are as much a symptom as a cause. It would also be a mistake, to put it mildly, for us to imagine that our obsession with the cult of physical perfection is wholly confined to our dogs.

Caroline Kisko, the secretary of the British Kennel Club, was recently quoted as saying that 'Celebrities, popular culture and fashion play a big part in today's society, and, unfortunately, dogs are not immune to our fickle tastes.' But fashion has played a central role from the very start of modern dog-breeding. The winners of conformation dog shows were never chosen purely because they were good herders, or excellent rat-catchers, or even because one could run faster than another.

It may be true that, when Paris Hilton appeared at the start of the current millennium with a tiny pooch in her handbag, registration of similar toy breeds soared. But the use of pet dogs as fashion statements or accessories is nothing new. In the fifteenth century, the English poet Geoffrey Chaucer wrote about a modish nun, a prioress who dressed in the smartest convent style, and who kept some 'smale houndes' close to her at all times. She hand-fed them on milk and sweet white bread, and Chaucer clearly meant her to represent a recognisable social type. Three centuries later, it is said that Marie Antoinette was still clutching her tiny lapdog, Coco, on the way to her place of execution. I should imagine that Coco's presence was unlikely to have endeared the Queen to the waiting tricoteuses.

At the start of the twentieth century, the celebrated actress Sarah Bernhardt used her elegant Borzoi hound to serve as a fashion prop, and when King Edward VII was seen in the company of his Irish Terrier, the popularity of that breed also spiked. The dapper red terrier was seen as the sort of no-nonsense dog that was suitable company for a man of his exalted station. Meanwhile, King Edward's wife, Queen Alexandra, carried around a small Pekinese, which helped to spark a fad among society ladies for that miniature breed.

When our distant ancestors first chose not to kill wolf cubs but to feed and take care of them, it is hard not to believe that at least part of the reason for that historic development was because the appearance of the cubs appealed to them. It also seems likely that Victorian gentlemen valued the looks of their hunting dogs almost as much as their abilities in the field. Even the Presbyterian minister Noble Huston, who detested dog shows and who claimed, in the best Calvinist tradition, to value the Red and White Setter on account of its admirable character, often commented on the great intrinsic beauty of his favourite breed.

It is not so much changing tastes in fashion that we should worry about, but the shrinking diversity within individual breeds. Ironically, while the number of recognised breeds has greatly increased in the past century, the internal variation of some of them has radically diminished.

Of course, some changes have been for the benefit of both dogs and their owners. Time has now dissolved some of the rancorous conflicts that featured in the stories of Irish dog breeds in the previous centuries. Thankfully, we have moved on from the period in Ireland's history that saw dogs poisoned, and hundreds of the houses where they were kept burned down. Many of the homes of the Irish gentry that escaped the flames are now run as hotels, or are occupied by the descendants of their former owners' tenants. In one sense, a similar process has taken place with regard to the gentry's dogs. None of Ireland's native breeds can be identified with any one social class in the way they could a hundred years ago. The Wheaten Terrier, for example, once worked as a farm dog that was used to kill vermin and hunt badgers, and was deemed best suited to those of a modest social status. Nowadays, Irish Wheatens are more likely to be seen taking their daily promenades along the broad avenues of Ireland's most affluent suburbs.

Some of Ireland's oldest breeds, like the Water Spaniel, are threatened with extinction, but at the same time, the Fédération Cynologique Internationale, the world governing body of dog breeds, now recognises hundreds of different varieties. While the ownership of pedigree dogs is still increasing, as Sean Delmar of the Irish Kennel Club pointed out to me, the availability of these new breeds has made the dog market much more competitive. That is particularly true for dogs at the bottom of the table of registered births. According to a recent analysis by Stanley Coren, the ten most popular breeds in the United States now account for more than half of all purebred registrations, while the fifty least popular breeds account for less than 2 per cent. That is not the only danger: the American Kennel Club acknowledges that the further dog breeds develop away from their original functions, the harder it is to protect those features that defined each breed in the first place.

In this context, it has become harder for some of the older breeds to survive, let alone compete. There is now much anticipation of which new types of dog will be revealed at shows such as the prestigious Westminster event in the United States. In the last few years, this event has welcomed such breeds as the Lagotto Romangnola (a water retriever from Italy); the Boerboel (a guard dog from South Africa); the Boykin Spaniel (a dog used to hunt wild turkeys in South Carolina); the Berger Picard (a herding dog from France); and the Bluestick Coonhound (a raccoon hunter from Louisiana). Knowledge of new and relatively obscure breeds like these can now be spread quickly through the social media, and they can gain sudden popularity. But those media can also be the means to draw attention to older breeds that are vulnerable, and which need to be protected if they are to survive.

New Tricks

While some traditional forms of employment for dogs have become redundant, it is also true that some new ones have opened up. Bloodhounds used to be the principal breed that was used in police and detective work, but now many other types of dog play a part. Several breeds are also called upon to act as medical response dogs, and even as canine therapists. The therapeutic powers of dogs was first realised during World War Two when an American doctor treating wounded and traumatised soldiers observed and recorded the beneficial effects that a small terrier called Smoky was having on them. Since then, the use of dogs in similar situations has greatly expanded, and dogs are now frequent visitors to nursing homes and hospices, and to children with physical or emotional difficulties. Indeed, it has also become a matter of routine in some parts of the world to send in a team of dogs after any natural or human disaster to comfort the victims and their families.

Medical response dogs can be trained to detect the blood sugar levels of someone with diabetes, and react when they become too high or low. If properly trained, dogs can also sense the approach of epileptic episodes, and carry medication or phones, or simply maintain a protective presence. There are recent reports that dogs can even be trained to detect the early stages of certain forms of cancer.

The involvement of some breeds with police forces, charity services and disability organisations has allowed greater monitoring of their DNA information, which has the added benefit of reducing the prevalence of inherited defects. Scientific research now holds out the possibility of solving some of the medical conditions that have arisen in some pedigree dogs in the past as a result of too much inbreeding.

A recent article in the *Scientific American* by Claire Mardarelli examined the case of the Dalmatian breed. The same genes that are responsible for that breed's signature spotted markings also produce high levels of uric acid in the Dalmatian's urine. This can cause urate crystals to form, and these often create very painful urinary blockages. There is one solution that is readily available: DNA analysis can identify the defective genes, and make sure that they are bred out. However, there is one drawback: selecting against uric acid also results in a spotless Dalmatian.

In 1973, Robert Schaible, a geneticist at the Indiana University School of Medicine, crossed a champion Dalmatian with an English Pointer, a breed with normal levels of uric acid, and with a comparable physique and disposition to the spotted dog. One of the litter that was produced by this union was subsequently crossed with another Dalmatian. Eventually, after fifteen generations of selective breeding, a litter with spots, but without high levels of uric acid, was born. And in 2011, the American Kennel Club allowed pups from that generation to register as purebred Dalmatians. This was the goal of the original project, and it shows that it is possible to combine the aesthetic appeal of a breed with a proper concern for its future health, even though, in this instance, it had taken thirty-eight years.

It seems possible that some of the medical problems that have tended to afflict some pedigree dogs may be eliminated, or at least substantially reduced, in the future through a similar approach. In July of 2016, seven Beagle and Cocker Spaniel pups became the world's first litter to be born by in-vitro fertilisation. The seven pups may all have come from the same litter, but they had different sires and dams. This occurred almost forty years after the first human birth from IVF treatment, but it still marked a scientific breakthrough, and it may suggest other ways in which some of the inherited problems faced by some pedigree breeds can be confronted and eventually overcome.

That might help, in turn, to dispel some of the fears of genetic defects in purebred dogs that have arisen in recent years, but of course it would not guarantee that all of the native Irish breeds will still exist in the future. The popularity of dog breeds can both rise and fall with remarkable speed. This can sometimes be triggered by specific events. In 1985, there were fewer than 7,000 registrations of Dalmatian pups with the American Kennel Club. That same year, the Walt Disney Company released a new movie version of *101 Dalmatians*, and the following year there were almost 43,000 registrations. By 1992, however, the number of registered Dalmatians had fallen back below 5,000.

In the case of this boom in Dalmatian numbers, the reason seems obvious enough: the Disney movie was hugely popular, and appears to have contributed directly to a sudden rise in puppy registration. However, other comparable spikes are more difficult to explain. In 1961, the number of Irish Red Setter pups registered with the American Kennel Club amounted to 2,546. By 1974, it had rocketed to 61,549. Ten years later, it had returned to the pre-boom level. Once again, a popular Disney movie that featured the breed, *Big Red*, had been released in 1962, and that may help to explain the initial surge in popularity. However, in this case the growth in numbers was sustained for well over a decade, and cannot simply be attributed to the impact of that one movie.

As Carol Beuchat of the Institute for Canine Biology has observed, the surges in popularity of one breed often seem to mesh with a drop in registrations of another. The Yorkshire Terrier, for example, went from 26,000 registrations in the UK in 1990 to only 5,000 a decade later. The Pug has gone in the opposite direction, from fewer than 1,000 in 2003 to around 8,000 within ten years. Clearly, fashions can change rapidly in dog ownership. However, there are also some long-term trends, and one of these is the sustained fall in the number of most terrier breeds, which is clearly a cause for some concern as far as the Irish, the Glen of Imaal, and the Kerry Blue Terriers are concerned. To return to the question I posed at the start of this book, if those breeds, or any other of Ireland's native dogs, become extinct, what would we have lost?

Rosa Cira has pointed out that many dog breeds were adapted, through deliberate human intervention, to conform to aesthetic standards that decreed that they should be a specified height, weight, shape and colour. Some of these standards were set on a fairly arbitrary basis, but many were based on a functional role that the particular breed of dog may no longer fulfil. Cira has suggested that, regardless of their origins, these breeds ought to be preserved as testaments to human ingenuity and achievement, and also as living specimens of the cultures that bred them.

In other words, the original purposes for which those dogs were bred may no longer exist, but they still connect our contemporary society with its past, and are valuable for that alone. Our native dogs may not be traceable in an undiluted bloodline back to the mists of Celtic antiquity, as some have believed, or have claimed to believe. It may even be true, as Michael Brandow has suggested, that our 'traditional' breeds are nothing more than 'commercial inventions of Victorian England'. However, there are several Irish institutions that also lay claim to be the direct heirs of ancient traditions that could, with equal justice, be described as the inventions of Victorian society. Besides, as I hope I have established in this book, the modern dog breeds that are native to this country have their own histories. By now, those histories span at least three centuries, not an insignificant stretch of time, and they are surely entitled to some measure of recognition and respect.

In the twenty-first century, dog-breeding has become an enormous, multi-national and self-perpetuating industry. Most of the world now lives in an era of post-functional breeds, and the forces that govern the economics of dog-breeding are increasingly hard to predict. There are very few breeds whose futures now seem entirely secure, and some or all of Ireland's native breeds may vanish, even in our lifetimes, if that is what contemporary needs and aesthetic preferences dictate.

Dogs still belong to just one species, *canis familiaris*, but they can range from breeds that weigh less than eight pounds to those that weigh more than 150. Some new types of dog, such as the Labradoodle or Cockapoo, are often dismissed as mere 'designer dogs', as if that indicated some newfangled and frivolous trend. But humans have been designing dogs since our ancestors first decided to bring a wolf cub back to the family cave. In fact, it is most unlikely that dogs would exist as a separate species nowadays if human beings hadn't intervened in their evolution.

Over thousands of years, we have bred dogs to hunt, to fetch, to track, to guard, to herd, to race, and to perform. They have been sent (on a one-way ticket) into space, and they have played a leading role in the detection of contraband drugs. We have even trained them to kill on our behalf. In some parts of the world they may still be used for some of their original purposes, but these days there simply aren't the same job opportunities for dogs in Western Europe. Instead, we have had to find new roles for most Western dogs, and that hasn't always been easy.

None of this is really the dogs' responsibility. We value them for their spontaneity and lack of inhibition, but we also require them to be docile and obedient. I can get annoyed when my dog, Cosmo, doesn't feel like fetching a ball I have thrown for him, and I have to retrieve it myself. But I can also resent Cosmo insisting that I should play with him when I want to read a book. At times I feel like his parent; at others, I feel that he acts like mine. These are, it seems to me, just the sort of contradictions that typify the human relationship with the canine species.

Perhaps the underlying reason for that relationship is that we don't just want dogs to be our friends; we expect them to act as our best friends. At a fundamental level, our intimate connection with domestic dogs is not replicated with any other animal. Dogs seem to lead lives that run parallel to, overlap with, and are complementary to our own. Our communication with them operates in a way that is quite distinct from our use of everyday language. Indeed, our emotional bond with dogs may even be predicated, in part, on their inability to talk back to us.

We are fortunate in Ireland to have nine exceptional and beautiful native breeds. There have been times when those dogs might not have considered themselves quite so lucky. There was a period when their pups were culled, their tails were docked, and their ears were cropped by their owners. That time is past, and each of the current Irish breeds has retained its own distinctive character—and so, of course, does every individual dog within each breed. They all come with a set of the emotional and social complexities that being a dog entails, and a big part of that involves their interaction with human beings.

That is a mutual exchange—even if it is often unequal. On one hand, humans nurture dogs; we feed and shelter them; we worry about their health; and sometimes intervene to save their lives through surgical procedures. We treat them as an integral part of the human family, and are even prepared to enter them in our TV talent shows. On the other hand, dogs also nurture us. They stand beside humans in our darkest hours; they serve in the front lines of our wars; they guide us when we lose our sight; they warn us of impending illness; and they rescue us from floods, avalanches and fires. They can even beat us in our own talent shows.

They might not understand all the words that we use, but dogs are very good at reading our emotions. I often look up to see Cosmo watching me intently—and unlike many other animals, dogs do not avoid direct eye contact with humans. It often seems when he is scrutinising me that he is trying to read every nuance of my body's language. And he can do that very well. When my mother died one Christmas, I felt that he could sense my sadness. He would sit beside me for long periods, resting his head on my lap, and his unobtrusive company was a source of great comfort to me. Cosmo invites me to interpret his moods just as he does mine, but he is much my superior in that regard. My failure to understand exactly what he wants must be a source of recurrent frustration for him.

In a founding text of Europe's classical literature, Odysseus returns to the island of Ithaca after an absence of twenty years. As he approaches his home, he finds his dog, Argos, lying abandoned on a dung heap. In his youth, Argos was celebrated for his speed, his strength and his beauty. But now he has grown old and weary, and is on the verge of death. Despite that, and unlike any human, he is still able to recognise Odysseus. Argos is too weak to rise to greet his master, but has just enough resources left to drop his ears and wag his tail. Odysseus is so moved by his dog's display of affection and loyalty that he cannot help but weep.

This is a small incident, only a moment, in an epic story of a terrible war and its aftermath. But that moment still conveys something of the deep connection, the intuitive recognition, and the unique emotional bond that has tied our two species together over thousands of years. We may live in a world where new types of dog are still being developed, and others are fast disappearing, but whatever future lies in store for Ireland's native breeds, I doubt if that fundamental bond will ever be broken.